ONCe UPON OUR PLANET

Written by
VITA MURROW

Illustrated by
AITCH

MAGIC CAT PUBLISHING

CONTENTS

ONCE UPON TWO SUNS
› 4 ‹

ONCE BEYOND THE NORTH WIND
› 10 ‹

ONCE UPON A SALT LAKE
› 17 ‹

ONCE UPON A MOUNTAIN
› 23 ‹

ONCE UPON A FOREST
› 28 ‹

ONCE UPON A PARADISE
› 36 ‹

ONCE UPON A SAVANNAH
› 44 ‹

ONCE UPON AN ISLAND
› 50 ‹

ONCE UPON A REEF
› 56 ‹

ONCE UPON THE TOP OF THE WORLD
› 62 ‹

ONCE UPON A TUNDRA
› 68 ‹

ONCE UPON A RIVERBANK
› 75 ‹

ONCE UPON TWO SUNS

Once amidst three seas, on land shaped by a broad crater, there stood a forest. Above the forest hung twin suns. Their fierce, unrelenting rays shone across the land, tormenting all those that lived in the forest below.

Within the forest, there could be found an ensemble of six players. One had a toothy grin. That was Crocodile. The second had floppy hair. It was Orangutan. The third wore a permanent necklace of bold stripes. That was Civet. The fourth had a most memorable profile. That was Proboscis Monkey. The fifth snoozed so much in the sun that an orange crest appeared on their chest. Sun Bear, of course. The sixth, and last, was a tiny but deft hunter. The ever-artful Leopard Cat.

THE SIX PLAYERS MADE UP THE CAST OF THE THEATRE OF THE FOREST.

The six players made up the cast of the Theatre of the Forest. The broad crater was their stage. Every day, the ensemble gathered to improvise, rehearse and dramatize. Their performances featured Sun Bear's feats of strength, Orangutan's dancing in the trees, Proboscis Monkey's comedic wit, and battle and chase scenes starring Civet and Leopard Cat. But best of all was the waltz of the Crocodile, a rapturous solo dance.

Crocodile's star act was equal parts comedy and tragedy. They swayed mysteriously, lulling their audience, then shocked them with sharp teeth and giant jaws! Yet just when the audience gasped, Crocodile would disarm them with a warm grin and silly swagger. The act received a standing ovation every time. It was delight for nearly everyone.

Everyone except for Crocodile. It wasn't the spectre of stardom that made Crocodile weary. It was the hot burn of the twin suns. Each moment on stage meant a while longer out of the refreshing river waters. Slowly, day by day, Crocodile's tough exterior blistered and peeled. Their eyes grew dry and stung. In the theatrical duel between Crocodile and the tyrant suns, the celestial twins never ceased to prevail.

One day, the players arrived at the Theatre of the Forest to find they counted a member too few. Their principal player, Crocodile, had not come. Oh where, oh where was Crocodile?

The ensemble rushed to the riverbank and called out. They looked for Crocodile's tail among the muddy ripples of the water. But they found nothing.

Sun Bear searched the forest floor, its trails and tracks. Civet carried questions of the missing animal to the quiet corners of the crater. Proboscis Monkey and Orangutan called out for Crocodile from the heights of the canopy overhead. Leopard Cat raced messages to the fast-moving rats and snakes of the understory. Sun Bear affronted every animal they encountered with a booming voice, "Have you seen Crocodile? From the theatre?!"

With no sign of Crocodile anywhere, the ensemble returned to the banks of the river, and stared down at the waters. And there, in the sand, they noticed fresh claw marks. They were the unmistakable shape of a crocodile claw. Hope alit their hearts! They followed the marks along the river's edge until they reached a pit of mud. Buried in the mud, crying quietly, they found Crocodile.

> "I'M TOO HOT TO WALTZ. MY SKIN IS TOO SORE TO SWAGGER."

"Dearest Crocodile," the animals pleaded, "we need you!"

"The show must go on without me," moaned Crocodile. "The twin suns have stripped me of my sway. I'm too hot to waltz. My skin is too sore to swagger."

The animals sighed. Crocodile didn't have fur, or dark hooded eyes, or any kind of protection from the hot power of the twin suns.

"I am weary. My head aches and my eyes are so tired," Crocodile croaked, and slipped into the mud below. The five players sat, confounded, along the riverbank.

"What are we to do?" asked Sun Bear.

"Well, there is only one waltzing Crocodile," mused Civet.

"Yet there are two suns," sighed Leopard Cat.

"Indeed," pondered Proboscis Monkey.

"Here's something to consider… " said Orangutan. "What if there were just one sun? Surely that would help poor Crocodile."

> "WHAT IF THERE WAS JUST ONE SUN? SURELY THAT WOULD HELP POOR CROCODILE."

The animals all looked at Orangutan.

"Civet and Leopard Cat, you are always pretending to battle," said Orangutan. "What if we entered a true battle… with the twin suns?"

Civet and Leopard Cat seized on the idea. "Yes, yes!" they cheered.

"But how can we reach them?" asked Proboscis Monkey.

Orangutan climbed high into a nearby tree and looked pensively at the twin suns. They sat on a loop of vine, like a playground swing, their fluffy legs kicked back. Then, with an impromptu *Zip!*, Orangutan shot out of the vine swing and into the air.

"We'll launch something at the suns," Orangutan announced, "with a swinging vine!"

Sun Bear and Proboscis Monkey sought out the largest rock on the riverbank. They rolled it towards the trees. Orangutan lowered the strongest and springiest vines down to Leopard Cat and Civet. Together, they fitted the vines into a long rope with a section in the middle, like a seat, where they loaded the big rock.

Finally, the stage was set for their great ambush. Leopard Cat and Civet held the vines taut and Orangutan and Sun Bear pulled the rock in its seat as far away from the trees as they could. They formed a giant slingshot, bigger than any myth or legend had pronounced before.

Proboscis Monkey rose into the trees...

"You there, golden suns!" Proboscis Monkey called.

"Come and have a look at something in the trees! The leaves are so dense, I need more light." The monkey beckoned, luring the suns down to where the slingshot lay in wait.

The twin suns crawled across the sky. They sunk towards the riverbank. Their colour changed from powerful yellow to a deep orange, and when they were as low as they could go, a blushing pink. As the two suns focused on Proboscis Monkey, the other players pulled the slingshot back. With one single chance, they released the mighty rock.

The rock sped through the air arrow-straight, its dense mass seemed light as a feather as it sailed towards the suns. The ensemble watched with anticipation. Would they strike the suns dead? Would the suns flee and change the sky forever?

What happened next, no one could have predicted. At the last moment, before the rock struck, one sun slid in front of the other. The rock slammed into the closer of two. The air around the animals cooled instantly. The sky across the crater transformed into a collision of colours: grey-blue at the edges and deep red at the centre.

The animals rushed towards the pulsing glow of the twin suns. And before their eyes, the sun that had been spared by the rock slipped out of sight. It cast a spray of pink and purple light as it disappeared. Then, the world around them became dark and cool.

The ensemble sat in awe on the riverbank, mesmerized by what they had witnessed, until their spell was broken by a sound as Crocodile emerged from their muddy refuge.

"Look!" the animals cheered. "We have slain the sun; it will torment you no longer!"

"Look yourselves!" Crocodile motioned to the new dark sky. In it sat the injured of the two twin suns. It was no longer blaring and yellow. Instead, it was cool and chalk white. Bruised slightly by the rock, but otherwise intact and, in fact, quite content.

From then on, instead of filling the sky at once, each twin had their own domain and their own name. One twin was still called Sun, they shared yellow light, bright and ablaze. The other twin was called Moon. They bestowed a dark blue hue, and were the bearer of cool airs and restful ways.

The players, too, took cues from the twins. The first five lit up the stage under the hot yellow Sun. Then, as Moon twin rose, Crocodile took to the stage. As cool and collected as could be, Crocodile danced and worked their magic... Until the curtain of night marked 'The End' of the show.

ONCE BEYOND THE NORTH WIND

Close your eyes and breathe. Imagine the air enters your body a cool drink and comes out a newborn snowflake. This is the air of Hyrea. A land high above us. So high, in fact, that to get there one must push past clouds to where the sun and moon have made an unlikely arrangement, rising and setting just once a year. Where waters have slowed to ice. A land guarded by Gryphons and home to Bo, the Wind Walker.

Bo was born and raised in Hyrea. With the annual cycle of the sun and moon, Bo mastered new things. Bo learned to forage, to fish and pick fruit. To cut timber and build. Bo learned to climb, to trek and skate, much like you and me. Yet one thing was strikingly different about Bo and her kin. They were as immense as the tallest trees, their feet great boulders with footsteps like thunder. Hyrea was a land of giants... and Bo, too, was a giant.

THEY WERE AS IMMENSE AS THE TALLEST TREES, THEIR FEET GREAT BOULDERS WITH FOOTSTEPS LIKE THUNDER.

Being a giant meant Bo could do amazing things. She could run fast and leap great heights. She could sculpt castles in the snow and grow plants in her hair. Most importantly, like all giants of her time and place, Bo could bring the secret gift of winter.

For years, the giants of Hyrea had been entrusted with bringing winter to the Southern Lands. Upon their fifteenth birthday, each giant took their turn as a Wind Walker and received the Map of the Elders.

The map directed the young giants on a trek across their kingdom towards Winter's Sea – the boundary with the Southern Lands. There, the Wind Walker would unleash a resounding breath, and bring winter to the lands beyond. It was an esteemed and vital duty.

> FOR YEARS, THE GIANTS OF HYREA HAD BEEN ENTRUSTED WITH BRINGING WINTER TO THE SOUTHERN LANDS.

Like those before Bo, winter lived hidden inside her, like a hibernating bear, until her fifteenth birthday. When the day arrived, Bo breakfasted at dawn, walked through the forest to stretch her giant legs, and enjoyed a treat of maple candy on ice. Upon returning home, Bo discovered the Map of the Elders on her doorstep. It was a scroll pinned with an icicle.

The scroll unfurled to reveal a large diagram that showed the land of Hyrea, a great ring of white and sparkle. Huge mountains on one side, a

voluminous river on the other. Beneath it all was the Winter's Sea – pure ice: a place of eternal winter. Underneath it all laid the Southern Lands. Throughout the map ran a path of red dots to mark the way Bo must journey as a Wind Walker. Just as generations of giants before her, Bo was to make the great trek to the edge of the Southern Lands and offer the breath of winter. It was critical — for winter allowed all things to reset, warm together and ready themselves for the grandeur of spring.

FOR WINTER ALLOWED ALL THINGS TO RESET, WARM TOGETHER AND READY THEMSELVES FOR THE GRANDEUR OF SPRING.

Bo set off, following the path on her map. She came upon high fortress walls that marked the boundary of Hyrea. Two majestic gates swung open and ushered Bo through. She followed the river to the south, the shadow of the mountains at her back. She looked over her shoulder once and nodded to the Gryphons that guarded over Hyrea before they went out of view.

The Map of the Elders was precise and had everything Bo needed. She gathered food along the way. She leaned birches to form shelter when she desired rest. And between brief moments of pause, her powerful legs propelled her on her climb. With Hyrea far behind her, Bo grew eager to see ice floes and glaciers ahead.

Yet, when Bo arrived at the edge of the Winter's Sea, the map began to fail her. Bo expected deep glaciers alongside a solid sea. The red dots indicated that all she would have to do was skate across the Sea's solid surface. But it wasn't frozen at all. It was milky and irregular. And the glaciers beside sported patches of green and brown mud, small grasses grew at the base.

Bo's heart beat hard. Her whole life had been leading up to this task: to glide across the Winter's Sea, fill her lungs with the breath of winter and deliver it to the Southern Lands on the other side. But the Winter's Sea had warmed, and the atmosphere seemed closer to spring than winter.

Nevertheless, Bo assumed the position. She straightened her form and slid a giant foot upon the sea. She longed to drift seamlessly across like a gentle swan, but instead she heard a crackling beneath her foot. Her heart sunk. As Bo shifted, her weight caused cracks to splinter at wild angles all around her. But she couldn't turn back. The Southern Lands needed her to deliver their winter.

Bo knew she would need to run. Bo summoned her courage and sprinted. With each step the sea cried out in crackly protest under her feet. Bo surged on and made it to the other side just in time to hear the ice break into large sheets behind her.

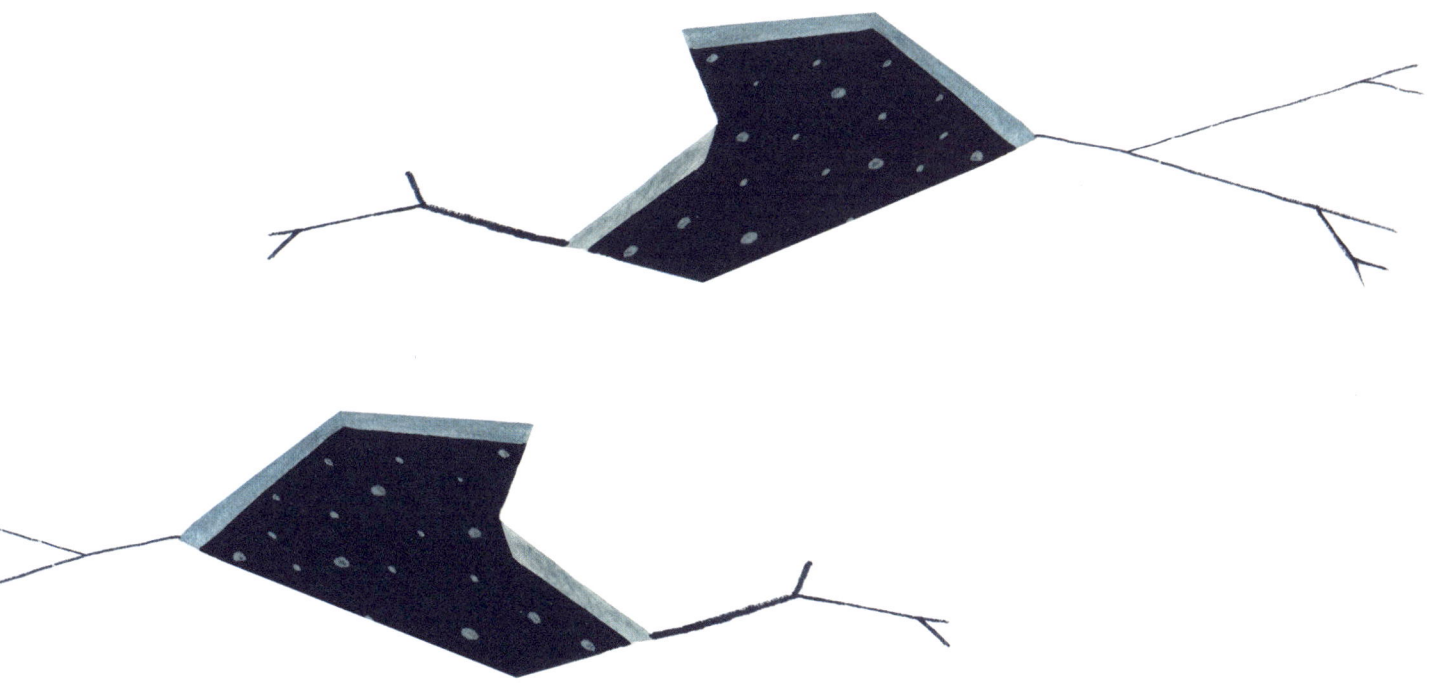

Bo stood at the precipice of the Southern Lands, autumn colours before her. She readied herself to fulfil her destiny, to offer the breath of winter and maintain nature's balance. She took as deep a breath as her lungs would allow, but when she exhaled, nothing happened. Bo tried again to rouse a cooling and wintry breath. A cool mist emanated, but no great flurry or frosty blanket as she'd hoped. Bo, having run across the Winter's Sea, was short of breath.

Bo, worried that she had failed her legacy, decided to return to Hyrea. She made her way back from whence she came. But where once had lain the frozen waters of the Winter's Sea, now lay an array of floating ice shards and swathes of open water. Bo knew something was not right. She needed to return to Hyrea to seek help.

> WHERE ONCE HAD LAIN THE FROZEN WATERS OF THE WINTER'S SEA, NOW LAY AN ARRAY OF FLOATING ICE SHARDS AND SWATHES OF OPEN WATER.

Bo tried to balance on two large planes of ice, but they quickly gave way and she was plunged into the chilly water. The force of her giant frame powered the water into a wave that rose well above Bo herself. The wave climbed and crawled across towards the shore where it broke powerfully.

The icy tidal wave sent a shower of ice crystals high into the air. The crystals flew so high that the Gryphons of Hyrea saw them shower the sky. Alarmed, the Gryphons spread their wings and leaped into the sky. They flew in a formation, soaring over the trek Bo had taken, to the spot in the Winter's Sea where Bo had begun to sink.

> THE CRYSTALS FLEW SO HIGH THAT THEY THE GRYPHONS OF HYREA SAW THEM SHOWER THE SKY.

The beasts lifted Bo to the surface and then into the air. They flew her safely back to Hyrea. As the Gryphons and Bo came into view, the giants of Hyrea assembled to learn what had become of their Wind Walker. They wrapped Bo in warm blankets and mosses, and set her by a fire. As she warmed, Bo recounted the puzzling shape of the Winter's Sea, and told how she was short of breath. The giants murmured and shook their heads.

"Why has the Winter's Sea grown soft?" the elder giants pondered.

"Has this ever happened before?" Bo asked.

Younger giants stepped forward and admitted that over the years they had noticed the Winter's Sea growing thin, and even heard sounds of ice turning into water.

Bo was determined to see her task through. But if crossing the melting Winter's Sea meant the loss of her own breath, how was she to blow winter to the Southern Lands? Then, Bo remembered the Gryphons. They had saved her, and this gave her an idea.

Preserving and sharing winter could no longer be a job for one, but for all of Hyrea. Instead of one Wind Walker, Bo suggested a fleet of Gryphons could carry a team of Wind Walkers. It would take a bit longer, but it would allow them to fulfil their promise.

> **PRESERVING AND SHARING WINTER COULD NO LONGER BE A JOB FOR ONE, BUT FOR ALL OF HYREA.**

And so it was, and has been ever since, that when a new giant comes of age in Hyrea, an army of giants takes to the air on a team of Gryphons. They fly from from their cherished kingdom, over their border land mountains, across the Winter's Sea and to the boundary of the Southern Lands.

They draw a communal breath, close their eyes and gently blow the quiet caress of winter over the domains. They bring the gift of rest to weary animals. They safeguard slumbering plants. And create a reason for gatherings and warm embraces for the community of the region.

> **THEY DRAW A COMMUNAL BREATH, CLOSE THEIR EYES AND GENTLY BLOW THE QUIET CARESS OF WINTER OVER THE DOMAINS.**

On their way home, the giants of Hyrea, and their guardian Gryphons, leave a trail of solar wind. The sky comes alive with colour, to remind the inhabitants of the Southern Lands of the magic of winter. And to inspire fortitude in the Winter's Sea, for so long as there is ice there, the Wind Walkers will never miss a visit.

ONCE UPON A SALT LAKE

It was dark inside the Monster's body. And very quiet. All that could be heard was a gentle *swish*, *swish*, *swish*. The sound of water lapping against the beast's sturdy ribs. Some called the monster Rahab, others called it Leviathan, some knew it as Tiamat. The beast went by many names, to many different people. All believed the creature to be of the salty water, of the abyss and dangerous.

Some said the Monster feasted on a whale a day. Others said it had a tail that led straight into its own mouth. One thing everyone agreed on was that to cross the Monster spelled doom.

The Monster jealously guarded a breath-taking city in magnitude and mystery. A city that lay secretly beneath the waves, made of glistening salt – the Crystal City. The tide rustled the crystals against one another, and the city made the sound of a million tiny bells.

The central arcade of the city was made of blue salt-crystal archways. Paths and byways ran out from the stunning centre. Every intersection was marked with a tall pillar.

The Monster patrolled the boundaries of the city. Their presence kept all the residents in and frightened guests away. So, the underwater city remained an obscure and unchanged place... Until one day, when new visitors arrived outside the Crystal City.

The visitors had heard tell of the terrible monster that guarded the Crystal City, but they were not deterred as it hissed at their approach.

The visitors ventured closer still and touched the salty walls. The Monster circled behind them, looking for a way to scare them off. Under their touch, doors — which hadn't been opened for hundreds of years — yielded their entry.

A powerful swell of water caused the visitors to surge forward and tumble into the city. The Monster's control had faltered. The inhabitants of Crystal City hurried to see what had happened.

The residents assembled to inspect the visitors, having never had any before them. They did not share language, but the visitors presented pieces of rock and minerals. They pressed these instruments into the salty walls and created drawings to tell their story.

The Crystal City dwellers were in awe. Some surprised, some curious, others frightened. Everyone watched spellbound. The story the visitors imparted was of a life on land, in a city not unlike the Crystal one. But the manner of life by the land dwellers had taken its toll and their land had become tired and vulnerable. One day, a punishing wave levelled their city. Their land, weakened by their way of life, gave way and plunged them into the water. It dealt the visitors a lesson they would never forget, and a drifting way of life they longed to put behind them.

The visitors bowed deeply to the inhabitants of the Crystal City, in a gesture that appealed for them to be taken in. The Crystal City dwellers were sympathetic and agreed that the visitors could remain in the city under one condition: they had to promise to live by taking only what they needed, and in turn sharing what they had to spare.

The Crystal City residents explained that one could borrow salt from the common areas if they needed it, so long as they returned it as soon as they felt they could. For this is how Crystal City had survived, cut off from the worlds above and below.

THEY LEARNED THE WAYS OF THE CITY AND WERE CAREFUL TO HONOUR THEIR PROMISE.

It was agreed, and the visitors joined Crystal City. They learned the ways of the city and were careful to honour their promise. They even added their own flair, decorating the city walls. Contentment reigned within Crystal City for everyone – everyone, but for the jealous Monster.

The Monster circled in the waters above and grew restless. As the citizens embraced their new life with the visitors, the Monster disapproved. The Monster was possessive and didn't like sharing. So, the Monster set in motion a sabotage.

Day after day, under the cover of night, the Monster scraped away salt from the great pillar at the city centre. At first, small holes took shape in the main pillar. Later the holes grew into great cavities.

One day, the central pillar was so weakened, it broke in half and crumbled right there in the main crossroads. The collapse sent up a puff of salt which sent alarm through the city. The watchful Monster grinned. Their plan was afoot.

All the inhabitants of the city, including the newest additions, gathered to inspect the damage. The Monster whirled above, a glowering cloud.

It peered down on them, imploring somebody to step forward to offer an explanation. But nobody moved. The Monster growled.

All in attendance agreed that the salt pillar was in ruin. This meant a direct betrayal of the spirit of the community. Had one among them broken the promise to their way of life? Mystery swirled. Who was responsible? Questions were raised. Was someone taking more than their share? Most importantly, fear was sewn. The inhabitants were frenzied.

Above them, the Monster was giddy. It watched the Crystal City face disquiet with glee. Only the Monster knew who the real culprit was. For it was their own claws that had stolen salt from the pillar.

To the Monster's surprise, the inhabitants of Crystal City did not turn on one another. They did not take the bait of hate. Instead, they met and decided the city no longer met everyone's needs. But because they were better together, they must take what they could and venture out of Crystal City to build a new home as one.

> ALL IN ATTENDANCE AGREED THAT THE SALT PILLAR WAS IN RUIN.

When the Monster saw their plans laid bare on the salt walls, they were furious. *How dare they leave!* thought the Monster. Wrought with failure, fury and force, the Monster unhinged its jaws as wide as a cave and plunged towards the Crystal City. In one swooping gulp, it engulfed the inhabitants.

The Monster zoomed at 100 knots, faster than the fastest marlin, its dizzying draft pulled the salt from its crystalline embrace and the city toppled into a powder. The finest powder rose to the surface of the lake where they formed ribbons of foam. The heavier powder coated the bottom of the lake and made a thick dark mud.

In the days and years that followed nothing or nobody returned to the lake. Nothing grew, grazed, drank or settled beneath or beside it. The lake lay desolate, an empty reminder of the fragile agreement between life and land, and the wrath of a jealous Monster.

> THE LAKE LAY DESOLATE, AN EMPTY REMINDER OF THE FRAGILE AGREEMENT BETWEEN LIFE AND LAND, AND THE WRATH OF A JEALOUS MONSTER.

As time passed the water met with warm air and the lake shrunk. As it did, its buried secrets were revealed. Tall, misshapen salt pillars rose on the perimeter, and not far beneath the lapping waves echoes of the archways, byways and crystal walls tie an ancient place to the present. But still deeper, lurks the Monster, ever watching, ever waiting to stir up trouble in the lake.

ONCE UPON A MOUNTAIN

Once upon a place where now stand the tallest peaks in the world, there swirled a boundless ocean. Its waters ruled over everything.

The ocean's tides governed time. The ocean's waves pounded everything in their path. The ocean's *crash!* was the most powerful sound of all. And the ocean's salt saturated the air.

The only body to share space with the ocean was the sky – and in it, two birds. A couple of white-capped water redstarts. They were plump and sweet birds who zoomed above the water in a lithe and easy manner. Their wings buzzed like kite tails on a windy day, a sound that zipped alongside the roar of the ocean.

THE WHITE-CAPPED WATER REDSTARTS WERE DETERMINED TO MAKE THEIR HOME AMONG THE FORCES OF THE OCEAN.

The white-capped water redstarts were determined to make their home among the forces of the ocean. Year after year, the couple sought tall rocks among the waves. There, they would build a nest of sticks and feathers. And within, the couple would lay a ring of blue eggs.

Sadly, every year, when the nest was unattended, the ocean waters would sweep the eggs out of the nest and into the waves. The tiny eggs never stood a chance. They sank like stones, their promise of new life quieted forever.

The white-capped water redstarts mourned and cried with sadness. Then anguish. Then despair. Each year, the birds poured their grief into the ocean. Yet the ocean took no notice of their sorrow. It just crashed its waves and rolled its tide.

On what would be the final chance for the white-capped water redstarts to have a family, they built their last nest. Before they laid their last set of eggs, they muttered a little prayer. In that prayer they pleaded to the great creatures of the region to protect the nest from the waters.

The white-capped water redstarts flew their prayer over the ocean to the place where shadows of the giant white-coated bears twisted beneath the waves. The couple skimmed low over the water, their insistent whistle ringing out.

Beneath the water, the bears heard the birds' searing cry. The intense, high-pitched sound cut through the muffle of the water. Their prayer pierced the bears' hearts. The white-coated bears surfaced and followed the birds as they flew to their nest.

The bears could see that the ocean's demanding waves splashed and leaped close to the fragile nursery. Witnessing the peril of the birds filled the bears with sorrow. They did the only thing they could do: they drank the waters in huge gulps to protect the birds, giving the unborn offspring their last chance at survival.

The white-coated bears drank and drank. They drew the waters of the ocean into their furry mouths until they were full to the brim. They guzzled until their bellies bloated with the sloshing salty mix of the ocean. Until all that was left of the ocean was a soft earthen bed.

And a bed was just what the massive white-coated bears needed! Their gorging had exhausted their giant bodies. They felt crowded with all they had consumed and they needed to lie down.

As the birds protectively warmed the eggs in their nest, the white-coated bears curled up in a furry pile on the dry ocean bed and fell fast asleep. The girth of the bears was immense. As they

snored and flopped in their slumber, a groove formed in the soft earth beneath them.

As the bears snoozed, their weight drove into the ground and they began to sink, like a footprint. The earth in return pushed back upon them. To stir the bears, the earth released small tremors. But the bears just shifted and nuzzled deeper into the earth.

A small fissure broke open beneath the bears. The fissure travelled in a long curving arc that wrapped all the way round. The bears simply rolled over, their sleep undisturbed.

The earth needed to let out a stronger message. It moved in a giant shift of weight that separated the land into big slices along the fissure. But the bears just lolled and rolled. One teetered precariously close to the edge of a deep crack.

The earth took offence at the loss of an ocean. The white-coated bears had become an immovable nuisance. It decided on a dramatic course of action to stir the sedated animals. It began with a shudder, but grew to a massive quake!

The earth wriggled and trembled, and it shook and rolled. It was as if the land had become one big ocean wave. But the bears slept so deeply the commotion hardly registered. The earth needed to transform itself. To change its shape entirely in order to wake the bears.

The earth let loose a final, powerful reel. It fractured a deep line that extended for miles. The land turned itself inside out. And earth's hidden depths reached to the sky in sharp spikes.

The rising of these peaks finally woke the bears. They stood on two feet and clung to the peaks with their legs. They held on for dear life as the earth took a different shape – a silhouette that now included a massive ridge that stood tall in the clouds. Its contours looked like giant teeth, higher and sharper than anything before and anything since.

To this very day, perched among these peaks are the white-coated bears. They snooze on rocks or splash in glacial pools. Shrouded in white, they are careful never to be seen and never again to disturb the earth.

The efforts of the white-coated bears are not forgotten though, for soaring above them, roosting at every height, can be found their friends, the plump and cheery white-capped water redstarts. They take to the skies by day with their sweet whistle of freedom. And by night, they cosy up safely in nests, beneath a sky lit with an ocean of stars.

ONCe UPoN A FoRest

Welcome to a forest unlike any other. One that spans miles and creates its own weather. Since its origins, this forest has lured many visitors in search of wonder, sustenance and adventure. Visitors are always welcome, as long as they are thoughtful. However, if they are caught stealing, or causing harm, they face well-founded consequences.

On a moonlit night, you can hear the Potoo Birds, phantoms of the treetops, as they recite the forest's cautionary tale. The Potoo Bird's yellow orb eyes transform into orange moons and their eery voices tell the tale of Captain Whitehead. It goes like this... Captain Whitehead was not always a captain. She was once just known as Monkey. She had a knack for tools and fixing things, and had a special way with plants. She bounded through the forest to offer her services as lookout, guide and helping hand. Her fluffy black coat made her appear more cuddly companion than warrior. But the hint of her ultimate calling was the monochrome helmet of hair that capped her square head.

ON THE DAY IN QUESTION, WHILE ALL LOOKED WELL AND GOOD, MONKEY SENSED SOMETHING WAS OFF.

Monkey held a special ability, which came to bear one auspicious day. It began like any other, Monkey was busy collecting rocks and sticks to make the tools she would need for the day. When she worked, Monkey talked to her materials.

"Your silky thread is so sturdy," she told the leaves as she wove them together. They responded by gliding into place.

"Your smooth surface will carve an easy path," she told the stones. They gave way with ease into points for cutting. You see, Monkey and her materials shared a language.

With her pack and axe upon her back, she perched in the tree canopy and studied the forest in search of small things she could fix and help with. On the day in question, while all looked well and good, Monkey sensed something was off.

She sniffed the air and found it smelled of grasses, fermented berries, water and sap. She also detected a hint of something unfamiliar.

Monkey listened then to the sounds of the forest. She heard the rustle of birds taking flight, and the patter of ground animals treading out. Yet, something else agitated the air.

She was about to go on her daily trip around the forest when she was approached by Poison Dart Frog.

"The ground is shaking and the leaves are quivering in our home," the frog stood in her way.

"Are there other places you can reside?" Monkey asked. The frog shook their head, "No."

"I'll go and see what I can find," Monkey comforted her amphibia-friend.

Monkey felt the ground and pressed on trees. Indeed, she too felt tiny vibrations.

Monkey laid down and asked the ground and trees for help.

"Please cease your trembling, do find your balance," she coaxed. The roots stirred beneath her and the earth softened at her gentle words.

Monkey set off to tell the frog that all was well but was interrupted by Anaconda and Jaguar who slithered and slunk up to her.

"What are you doing out?" Monkey asked. "You're normally tucked away in a cool and dark place during the day."

"We can't sleep; it's much too bright," explained Anaconda.

"We are missing the dark shade in our part of the forest," Jaguar complained.

"Missing?" Monkey was alarmed. She sped high into the trees and swung along the tops until she reached the area where Jaguar and Anaconda made their home. To her surprise, there was a gap in the forest: an empty space where light poured in.

Monkey spoke to the trees. "Can you fill the gaps?" she appealed.

The trees stretched their branches and filled the void. Anaconda and Jaguar headed back to rest. Monkey's morning had been unexpectedly full. With so much excitement she had nearly forgotten about the oddity in the air.

Then, Monkey passed beneath a majestic old tree. She heard voices above.

"The noise is so loud I can't hear my own thoughts!" Sloth fretted, their claws scratching in despair.

"The racket is bothering me too," Tamarind confided to Sloth.

"What noise?" Monkey asked, stopping beneath the pair. They gestured up to their gnarly part of the tree. Sure enough, as Monkey arrived at their roost, she could hear a sound too. It was a grumbly-rumbly-hungry-stomach sound, the likes of which could only have come from the stomach of something fierce.

Monkey was vexed. She wanted to ease the burden for Sloth and Tamarind, but a sound wasn't something she could correct by asking the natural world for help.

Higher aloft in the tree, Macaw and Toucan were deep in debate. Monkey swung up to see if they could help.

"Friends, are you hearing a sound?" Monkey inquired. "A rumble, a din, that is shaking the ground?"

"Oh, that?" said Toucan. "It's coming from the Beast!"

"A Beast?" squawked Macaw.

"I saw it with my own eyes," insisted Toucan.

"I'll go investigate," said Monkey, and off she went.

> IT WAS A GRUMBLY-RUMBLY-HUNGRY-STOMACH SOUND, THE LIKES OF WHICH COULD ONLY HAVE COME FROM THE STOMACH OF SOMETHING FIERCE.

The image of Frog on the uneasy ground, the thoughts of Anaconda and Jaguar lying awake, the appearance of Sloth and Tamarind – so agitated – and the voices of Macaw and Toucan spurred Monkey on.

Monkey wound her way to the edge of her territory. It was the threshold of a cliff that dropped to a different section of forest. But when she looked over the cliff, no forest could be seen. Instead, emptiness lay before her. Monkey was aghast to discover this injury to the forest. A haze of smoke clouded Monkey's vision and the rumble was louder.

AT HER CALL, VINES CREPT DOWN THE CLIFFSIDE. LEAVES COLLECTED IN A NEAT PATH AND LONG, STURDY BRANCHES LOWERED TO HEM THEM.

As the smoke cleared, two weary-looking animals came into sight – Capybara and Tapir. Tapir was carrying Capybara, who looked unwell.

"Neighbours, what's befallen you?" Monkey called down.

"The Beast has eaten our part of the forest," coughed Capybara.

"Can we come up to yours?" implored Tapir.

"Of course!" called Monkey urgently. But they were too far to reach. She looked around for something to help them climb up, but there was nothing to be found.

She took to the forest floor and summoned her friends, the trees, plants and leaves. With kind and clear instruction, she asked the forest for its help. At her call, vines crept down the cliffside. Leaves collected in a neat path and long, sturdy branches lowered to hem them.

The natural materials formed into a narrow suspended bridge. It cascaded from Monkey's forested area to the barren patch far below. Though the bridge was steep and perilous, Tapir and Capybara had no alternative but to trust its strength. Careful not to look back at the destruction behind them, the two animals ascended the woven vines until slowly, gingerly, they had climbed to safety.

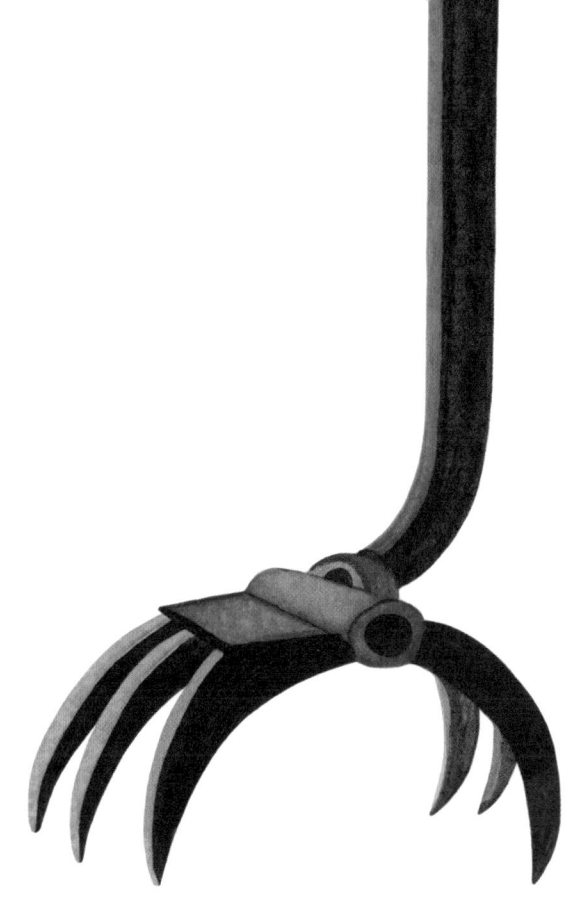

Monkey embraced Tapir and helped Capybara down. As she ushered the animals towards the protection of the trees, the ground beneath her gave an unearthly shudder. A roar surged behind her. And Monkey turned to meet a terrifying sight. A looming, glinting behemoth was advancing straight towards the bridge. It was the Beast!

Monkey urged the animals forward, away from danger, but she did not follow them. Instead, she walked towards the object of terror. She squared her small body atop the bridge.

She saw that to stop the Beast from claiming her part of forest next, she must sever the bridge. She extracted her axe and was ready to defend her territory.

MONKEY STRUCK THE BRIDGE WITH ALL HER STRENGTH. ITS VINES WRITHED AND TWISTED AS THE BEAST ADVANCED.

Monkey struck the bridge with all her strength. Its vines writhed and twisted as the Beast advanced. Monkey chopped and hacked, trying to bring it down before the Beast could climb aboard, but the bridge refused to cede. It was impressively strong. But so was the Beast, it rolled forward and barred its shiny teeth.

In a final move of desperation, Monkey dropped to her belly. With her eyes closed, she focused all her might on the bridge — which she herself had summoned into being to bring safety to her friends — as it now threatened to help her enemy. Monkey took a deep breath and asked the bridge to cut itself loose.

MONKEY TOOK A DEEP BREATH AND ASKED THE BRIDGE TO CUT ITSELF LOOSE.

▸ 3 3 ◂

As she knew was inevitable, the Beast boarded the bridge. The monstrosity snarled as it came towards Monkey, threatening not only her own life, but the very existence of her forest. Had Monkey's plea been heard? A terrible creaking emanated from the bridge; it grew louder with every snarl of the Beast.

Then, suddenly, under its girth, the bridge began to unravel. As Monkey jumped free, the bridge untangled its vines, let go its leaves, retracted its branches and – with a monstrous screech of colliding metal – discarded the Beast to the barren lands below.

Safe beside the other animals, Monkey watched a cloud of dust rise from the ground. A terrible *Boom!* followed, announcing the triumphant defeat of the Beast. The animals of the forest sent up a cheer. They lifted Monkey high in the air.

"Our Captain!" the animals announced victoriously.

From that day forward, when Monkey made her rounds as helper of the forest she was greeted with, "Good day, Captain Whitehead." When animals saw her bobbing through the branches, or dancing along the forest floor, they were comforted for they knew their home was protected.

As the years passed, the destruction of the Beast was replaced by new growth, and this story was committed to memory in the languages of the forest. When the moon is high, any visitor nearby can hear the Potoo birds retell the tale so as never to forget the legacy of Captain Whitehead.

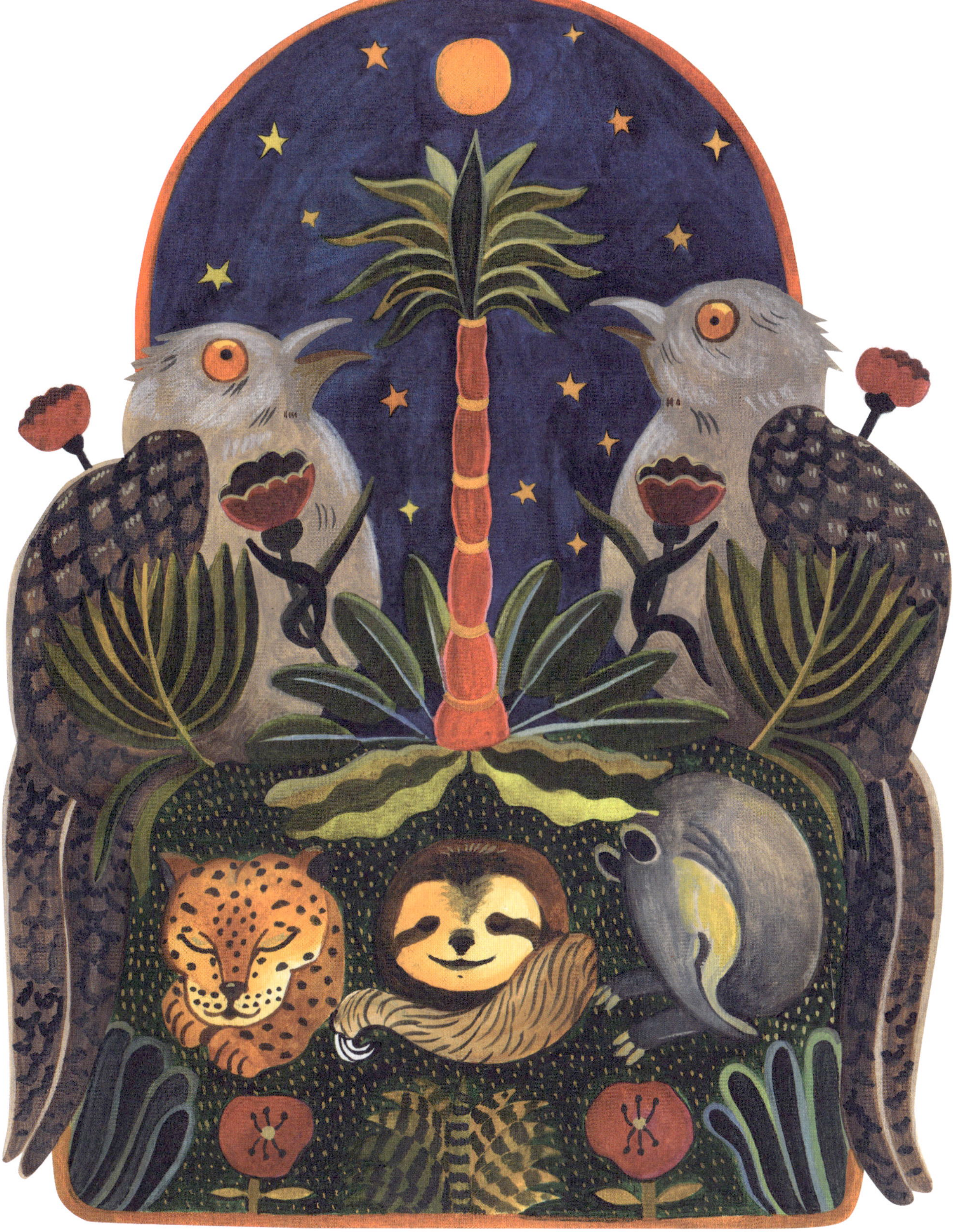

ONCE UPON A PARADISE

Long ago, before there were plants or animals, before there was ocean or land, there was one thing: *Darkness*. *Darkness* was rambling, it was consuming, and it was quiet. *Darkness* permitted nothing. Not even a speck of dust. And the world was rather boring. It lacked contrast and eventfulness, rhythm and joy. So *Darkness* called upon a friend. This friend's name was *Light*.

Upon invitation, *Light* arrived with a subtle approach. It began a tiny pinpoint and gently expanded into a ball. The ball glowed brightly and found itself a spot to rest. The bright bundle *Light* and *Darkness* shared the world like old friends.

Darkness and *Light* determined a pattern of rotation so that they would each be in charge, part of the time. It was an amiable dance and the goodness they offered one another brought other good things into being – so much goodness that a paradise was born.

With the new balance of *Darkness* and *Light*, things that had once been frozen began to thaw. Large ribbons of the world that had been black and icy turned blue in colour and liquid in texture. Soon, great oceans came into being.

From large areas of water rose small patches of earth that reached for the light. When light showed on these isles, plant life began to grow. Great green towering plants with generous flowers, blossoms and seeds. Below the water plants grew too. In a fringe around the isles, fuzzy coral took shape. It branched and carved its tentacles around the isles... Until it became a mighty reef. And with each new growth came a Spirit to guide it.

THE SPIRITS WERE STEWARDS OF THE NEW LIFE AND EACH TENDED TO ITS DUTY WITH CARE AND REVERENCE.

A Spirit of the reef, a Spirit of the shoreline, Spirits of the hills and forests. The Spirits were stewards of the new life and each tended to its duty with care and reverence. They made sure each new living thing in paradise had light, air and nutrients. They made sure there was harmony.

This wasn't always easy, because of one Spirit in particular, whom the other Spirits called 'May', as in, *May we know your purpose?* You see, May was the Spirit of a strange new thing. The thing was the

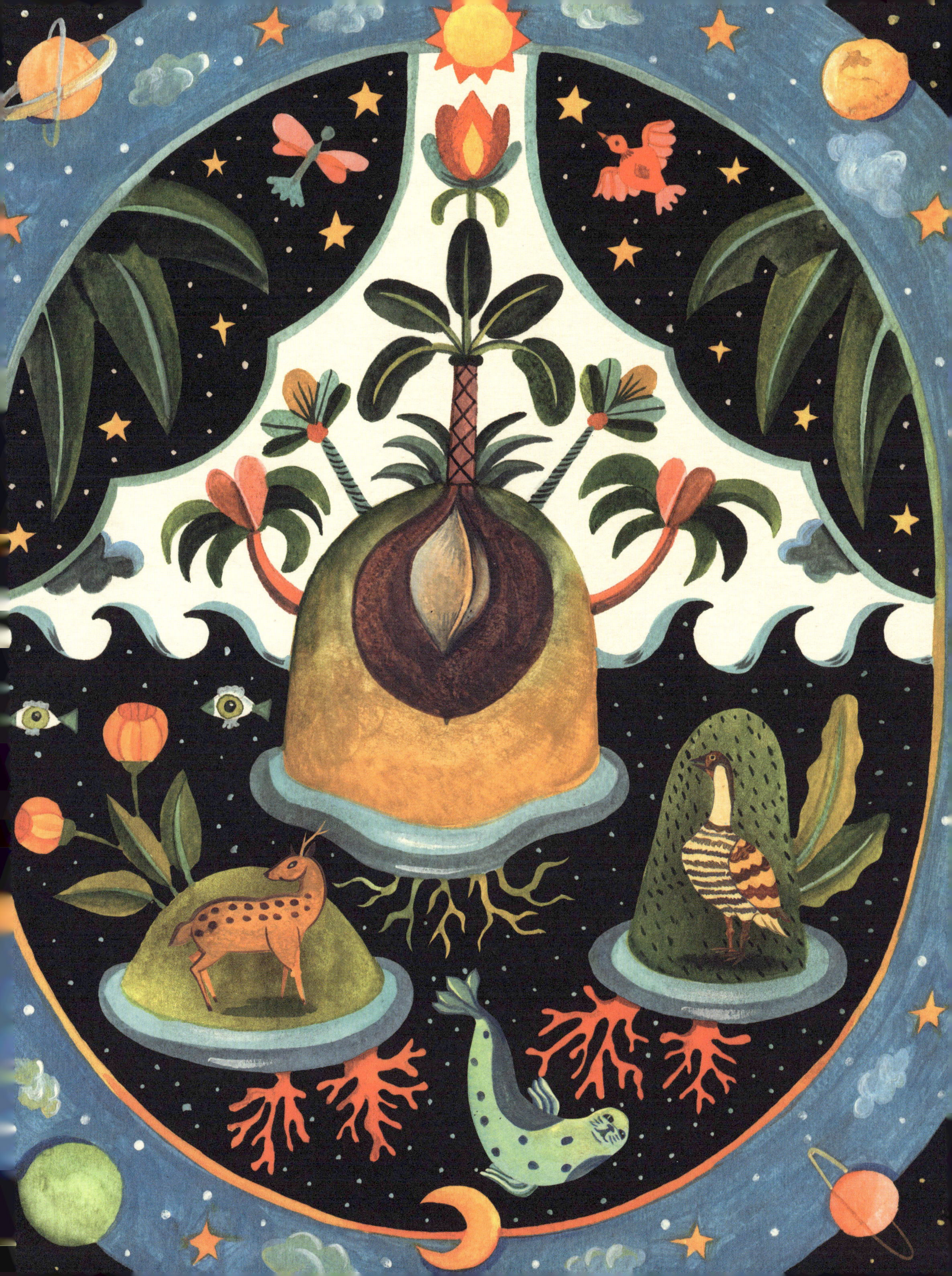

size and shape of an oblong ball. It was hard to determine its purpose in the paradise.

May the Spirit was also a little irregular. Unlike the other Spirits, who tended diligently and seriously, May was silly and wanted to frolic and play pranks. Once May dammed up a stream with rocks so the forest Spirits had to visit a rushing waterfall to help their plants. Another time, May swapped the direction and location signs the Spirits had put in place to guide their way in the ever-changing landscape. May turned each one around. Confusion abounded. The Spirits were not amused; while they were busy working, May was up to mischief! And so, the Spirits began to ignore May.

May began to feel left out. May pouted, stomped and sulked.

"I'll show them!" May said, and dug a great pit in the sandy soil. May raised their oblong ball high and the air and proclaimed, "My charge, your misery confounds me!" And with great drama, May placed their oblong ball in the pit and buried the curious object.

To mark the spot, May crafted a big sign that read: 'YAM!' For May insisted on being silly even in the signing of their very own name. All the other Spirits rolled their eyes.

"What could May be up to now?" the Spirits murmured. Yet they were mostly glad it wasn't a bother to them. Little did they know, with this one final prank, May had set in motion a great change that would mark their paradise forever.

As the pattern of *Darkness* and *Light* continued, days passed into months, then years, then eons... and along the way, the land and water transformed. The plants bore fruit and nuts, and the reef stretched for miles. The waters swarmed with life as sea creatures grew to throngs of fish and aquatic animals. Immense trees, sumptuous grasses, blossoms and vines covered the land, and even covered up May's sign.

In the trees, winged animals came to roost, and beneath them bugs and insects created busy pathways. The Spirits watched on contently, until one day, a new creature arrived... Tall and two-footed, it was curious and crafty, and it was hungry!

THE SPIRITS WATCHED ON CONTENTLY. UNTIL ONE DAY, A NEW CREATURE ARRIVED...

The new addition drew fish from the sea and gobbled them up. The same creature shook fruit from the trees and chewed it down. And soon beside it stood more and more of the same creature in all shapes and sizes.

The two-footed creatures began to make camps. They bent branches for shelter. They cut grasses to make pathways and moved materials from the lush areas to beaches. They made rafts so they could occupy both the water and the land. It was thrilling for the Spirits, who excitedly revealed to the two-footed creatures all the features of their paradise.

The two-footed creatures sensed the Spirits and

left little gifts for them. All the Spirits except May, for May hadn't yet shown the new creatures anything to be grateful for. When the two-footed creatures came across the sign saying 'YAM!', they laughed. What use could such a strange and funny-sounding thing be to them? And so they forgot May and their sign, leaving no gifts behind.

One day, upon a raft, a great many two-footed creatures arrived. At first it was exciting. The creatures disembarked and greeted one another. There were offerings of foods and merriment. But as the days wore on, it became clear there were not enough fish in the waters or fruit in the trees to feed all of the new inhabitants. The creatures gobbled everything up quickly, before the Spirits could replenish the ocean or sprout new nuts and berries.

The Spirits were worried. The two-footed creatures were worried. But May had no interest in worry. May was just bitter. No one had discovered May's secret gift buried in the ground; May had received no attention or special gifts. No one appreciated their humour, their nature, their zest.

THE CREATURES GOBBLED EVERYTHING UP QUICKLY, BEFORE THE SPIRITS COULD REPLENISH THE OCEAN OR SPROUT NEW NUTS AND BERRIES.

So May threw a tantrum, commanding the elements to produce a storm. The sea life fled their homes for the unknown. May's rage grew until it was out of control, matched by the winds and the rain.

SO MAY THREW A TANTRUM, COMMANDING THE ELEMENTS TO PRODUCE A STORM.

The two-footed creatures huddled in their shelters. Together with the Spirits they watched in pain as the greenery and flowers were overcome with water, torn and strewn about. Wind hammered the shoreline and sands rose into swollen dunes. The reef abraded. The sea life left their homes and floated away into the unknown.

When the storm ceased, the two-footed creatures and the Spirits took store of their paradise. The isle had changed dramatically. It was no longer a place of harmony, richness, food or fish. It looked bleak. The waters had overtaken the shoreline. The sands had reshaped the reef. And the trees were naked.

The two-footed creatures set about clearing debris to make a raft to sail away. The Spirits could see right away that it would take many cycles of light and dark before their paradise could be restored. With little shelter and no food, the isle wasn't going to be a welcoming home to anyone. The Spirits set to work straight away. All except May. Everyone just glared at May.

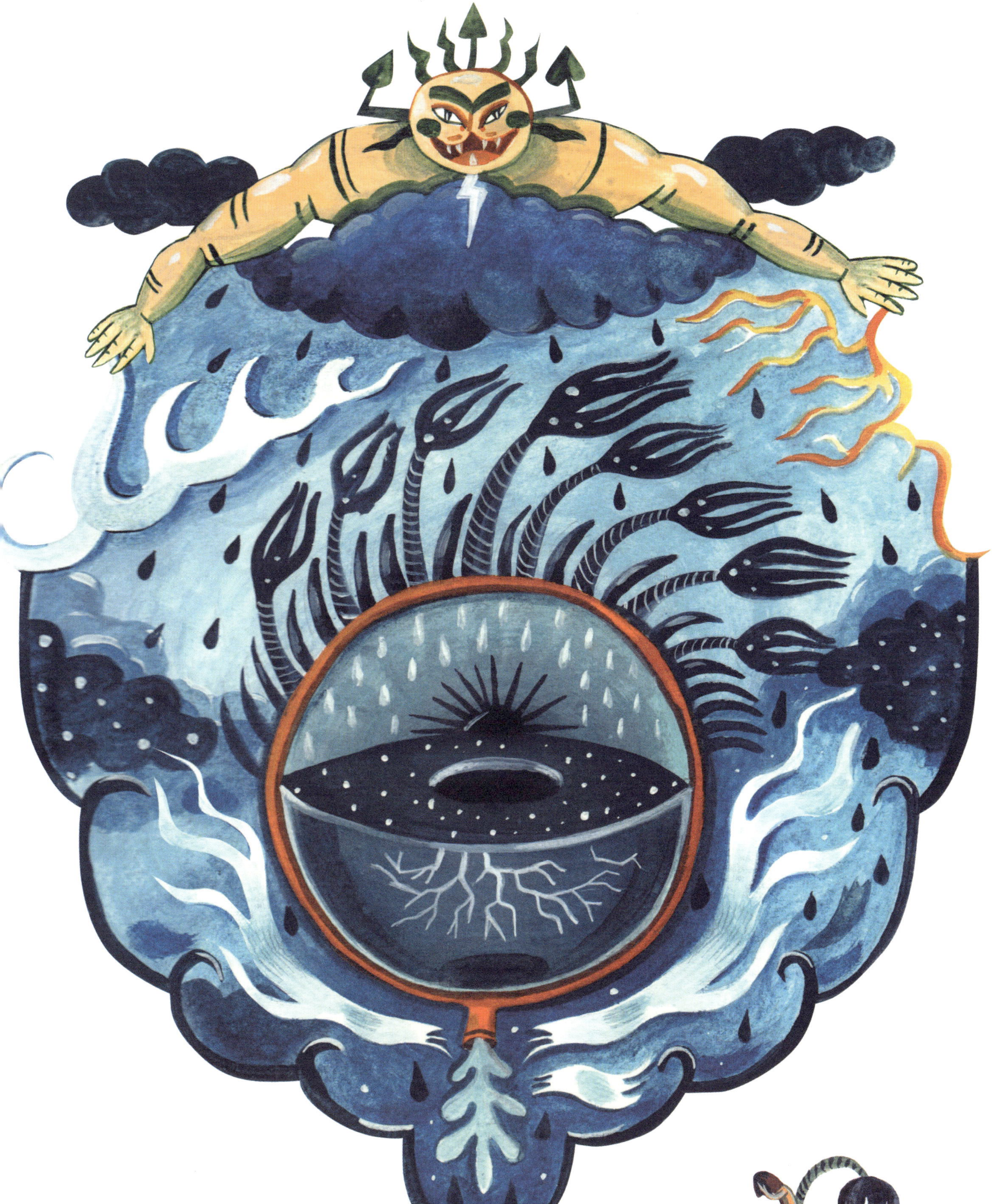

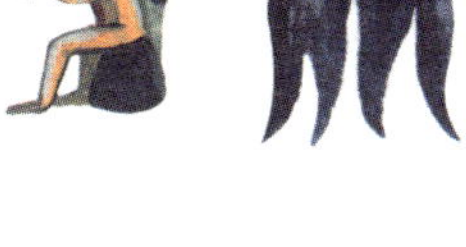

May felt sheepish. They moped in remorse but none of the other Spirits felt sorry for them. And it didn't make them feel better either. May moved to the beach and watched as the two-footed creatures boarded their raft. There wasn't enough room for all of them and a few smaller ones were left behind.

May's heart broke for the little ones. And at once they stopped feeling sorry for themselves. Instead, May turned their effort to recovering from their mistake. May paced and paced and soon arrived on the spot where they had buried their object for safekeeping. Littie did May know, behind them trailed the little two-footed creatures that had been left behind.

May watched on with surprise as the two-footed creatures gathered around the sign that read 'YAM!' The two-footed creatures inspected it with curiosity and then noticed that beneath their feet the soft soil had slid away in the storm. There, peeking out, was an end of the strange object May had buried. May watched on in wonder.

The two-footed creatures pried the object from the soil and turned it in their hands. They pressed it and caressed it. They smelled it and probed it, and their eyes lit up with possibility. May watched eagerly as the two creatures carried the strange object to the shoreline. They jumped up and down and waved the thing in the air. May was in awe.

Then, May watched as the two-footed creatures warmed the beach with a blaze and buried the object beneath the smouldering earth. After such time as they deemed it ready, they extracted it from the embers, unrolled it and inhaled the delicious smell of cooked food. And then, the two-footed creatures feasted.

The two-footed creatures treated the yam with delicacy and reverence, taking off small bites and sharing it so each one of them could benefit from the feast. May was filled with joy and purpose. And saw, finally, their important role in paradise.

From that time onward, the two-footed creatures left gifts at the place where the yam had been found, and May was so humbled. May continued to bury their special prize: the yam, which kept the two-footed creatures happy, healthy and thriving.

Renewed once again, the two-footed creatures could set to work taking care of the isle. Slowly they helped the paradise, and its Spirits regrow and generate; the flora and fauna, the fish and the coral… and most of all the precious yam.

For as long as they kept the plants and their Spirits in harmony - the two-footed creatures could call the beautiful isle their home.

ONCE UPON A SAVANNAH

Imagine an enormous open space, serene in sound and neutral in colour. Once an expansive forest, time has transformed it into an uninterrupted grassland. This is the savannah. At first, it presents itself as still and quiet. The swaying of grass the only sound. But upon careful listening, one may hear the muffled footfalls of a mighty cat, the gentle crunching of a leathery creature lunching, or even the sneak of a snake slicing through the grass. Or, most importantly of all, the gentle rhythm of rain, and the swish of water flowing into pools and drinking holes for the residents of the savannah.

Vital showers of rain connect the savannah to a wide sky full of activity. A multitude of stars by night, a bath of sunlight by day. And two old friends who share the skyscape — Thunder and Lightning. This is their story.

Most relationships experience moments of tension, struggle or discord. Being in a friendship sometimes means one must 'weather the storm'. The bond between Thunder and Lightning was no different.

Thunder was built of a soft and formless material. A puff that took on many shapes. Thunder enjoyed mimicking the shapes found on the savannah. Sunshade-shaped trees, long-necked animals, humped beasts and spiky long reptiles. It was easy for Thunder to play around with their form, for their only mass was a well of water, which they nestled and protected in a bubble close to their heart.

THUNDER WASN'T ALWAYS CERTAIN OF THEIR FEELINGS OR WHAT THEY WANTED.

Thunder had the unique ability to permit this well of water to flow free on occasion, in the form of a rain shower. They would look down at the savannah below and if they noticed a dry spot or a section lacking in creatures or plants, they would share their water in a quick burst, sometimes leaving a signature rainbow in their wake.

Thunder was of a docile nature. Thunder said, "Sure," or "Yes!" even if they weren't sure or didn't really feel in agreement. Thunder wasn't always certain of their feelings or what they wanted. And seeing as their only companion in the sky was Lightning, a being who almost always was knew their mind, Thunder deferred to them.

Lightning beheld a confident and intense personality. They were always first to appear, quick to speak up, and had a crisp and sharp tone, which meant they nearly always got their way. Every reaction from Lightning was a strong one. If they were hot – *BAM!* – sparks would shoot out from their centre. If they were irritated, they would lash out – *ZAP!* – even if it hurt the feelings of Thunder.

With Lightning never far, Thunder's control over the rain didn't last long. Lightning would boss Thunder around, telling them when to produce the rain – or not.

THUNDER COULD NEVER MATCH LIGHTNING'S FLASHY DOMINANCE.

"Drop the water now, Thunder!" they would command. And then Lightning would put on a great show of lights. Even though Thunder felt pushed around, they would yield and let the rain fall. Thunder could never match Lightning's flashy dominance.

Lightning used other means to get their way too.

"Look!" they'd point out. "Those beings are growing something in this odd spot. You should drop rain there!"

▸ 45 ◂

Thunder would look at the work of the beings and wonder, *Is this a lasting spot to grow things? I don't usually offer rain here, because it just rolls away.* Thunder preferred to bring rain in patterns that they could keep track of. They didn't like to be told *when* and *where*, but Lightning was forceful and Thunder found it hard to refuse.

And so, alas, Thunder would say, "Sure," even if they weren't sure.

Lightning compelled Thunder with their vanity too.

"That lake is too shallow, I need to be able to see my sparks more brightly. Maybe you should fill it up?" Yet it wasn't really a question.

"Okay," Thunder conceded.

Sometimes Thunder would grumble to themselves, but it didn't make them feel any better.

Instead the only thing Thunder felt was sadness. Over time, Thunder grew very sad indeed. Until one day, Thunder felt so fragile that they tightened the hold around their sacred water and drifted to a far corner of the sky.

The savannah below took notice. The beings, creatures and plants who dwelt there gathered and looked to the sky for signs or sightings of Thunder's cloud. Those that could, moved closer to the lakes, rivers and trees. Beings collected the water in vessels and in leaves. Animals grew tired from thirst, and instead of hunt or play they laid down for long rests.

THE WET SPACES SHRANK, AND THE SOIL CHAPPED AND RIPPLED.

The wet spaces shrank and the soil chapped and rippled. Soon animal families and groups of beings grew smaller. The plants they sheltered under and ate from were no longer shady and green, but brittle and spare. When new little shoots didn't appear with the new season, change was imminent.

Without hope of seeing rain again, the animals and beings left their dens and clearings and marched away, leaving barren holes and empty containers behind. Their faces and forms trudged towards a new and uncertain home. Thunder watched from their hiding spot in the far corner of the sky. A great sadness and disappointment came over them.

Lightning watched the change too. Even though they had not spoken for some time, Lightning knew it was time to talk to Thunder.

When night fell, Lightning tried to get Thunder's attention by putting on a show. Lightning lit up the sky with heat and electricity. Lightning's energy drowned out the brightest stars — their long white arrows turned the night as bright as day.

All this bluster pushed Thunder towards a new feeling. Anger. Anger at Lightning for being so pushy and angry at themselves for not having stood up to Lightning. Thunder was ready though, and hoped upon hope, as they watched the last animal shrink from sight, that it wasn't too late to act.

But behind Thunder, something dangerous had happened. Lightning's light show had consequences beyond anything they had imagined. One of their white arrows had struck the savannah and the tall, dry grasses had caught a spark. As they swayed, smoke bloomed from their tips. The smoke took shape and became a blanket. The blanket covered the grassland quickly and beneath it, the glow of a fast-growing fire lit the smoky blanket from behind. It looked, from above, like a phantom with a million orange eyes staring at the sky. Lightning looked down in horror at the monster they had created.

Thunder burst forth from their corner of the sky and charged at the orange-eyed smoke blanket. Lightening watched and saw for the first time that in power and might, Thunder was their equal. The very same Thunder who had always said "Yes" and "Sure" was transformed.

Lightning beheld a Thunder that was utterly in control, who was self-assured in the face of danger. Lightning was humbled and nodded to Thunder in a gesture of respect. Lightning made room for Thunder.

It was Thunder who took centre stage in the sky and, with an earth-shaking boom, cleared the air and made way for a wave of water. The rain Thunder welcomed fell in a long, wide ribbon from one side of the savannah to the other. It fell in mists and deluges, sheets and sprinkles.

The rain filled the pools, lakes and vessels. The water rewrote the land until once again it looked like a home. New passages and plateaus were carved for plant and animal habitats. The waters reached the feet of the retreating animals and beings. They turned just in time to see the savannah restored to a place of possibility.

> **THEY SAW THAT TOGETHER THE FRIENDS SHARED A POWER SO STRONG IT SUPPORTED THE VERY BALANCE OF THE SAVANNAH.**

Thunder saw the power in their own voice. They saw the return of plants, animals and beings, and knew something had to change between them and Lightning. With the gentle pitter-patter of rain beneath them, Thunder asked Lightning to promise each day to listen to one another. Lightning understood they had hurt Thunder. They were glad to see their friend at their side. Lightning agreed at once to do better. They saw that together the friends shared a power so strong it supported the very balance of the savannah.

As long as the rains fall, the grass flourishes and the animals make the savannah their home, you can be sure the friends have kept their promise. If the lands become dry and the sky grows empty, we must look to the bonds between ourselves and ask whether we have set a good example to our two friends in the sky. Have we honoured our hearts, used our voices and lived in the spirit of friendship?

ONCE UPON AN ISLAND

Locate in your mind a place where curving sandbanks give way to tranquil seawaters. Where a crop of islands is spread wide. Atop these islands position abiding towers: coconut trees. For generations, these islands have endured rains that saturate, waves that carve and winds that test. In a constant state of transformation, these islands will someday yield to the sea. Therefore, existence has long been a topic of discussion here. This is one such conversation.

Once upon and island, there were two coconut trees. They craned over the turquoise waters. One was tall, the other short. On a hot and gusty day, as heavy clouds rolled in the distance, the tallest of the trees turned to the smallest.

"I suspect this next storm will be my last," the tall tree, named Hassan, sighed.

"Your last?" the smaller tree, called Sitha, asked, aghast.

"As days wear on, we coconut trees are less and less appreciated," Hassan explained.

"What do you mean?" Sitha asked her elder innocently. For she saw their world through fresh eyes. Her fronds were bright, and she was without the flowers of a more seasoned tree.

"Once, we were everything here," the big tree said, slumping their leaves towards the water. "Look around, little Sitha. Now we are just part of the background."

Sitha saw that some guests of the island, who dwelt in tall boxes, who arrived on watercrafts and air machines, frolicked along the sandy circumference and paid them little regard.

"We have been reduced to 'just a place to hang a hammock'," Hassan lamented.

Thunder emanated from beneath the dark clouds. The sky mirrored Hassan's mood.

"The end is near for me," Hassan brooded. The elder tree released a loose coconut with a thud.

Sitha worried for her elder. Hassan had guided and protected her. Some of her roots were even entwined with his. She wanted to reassure him and stretched her

> THUNDER EMANATED FROM BENEATH THE DARK CLOUDS. THE SKY MIRRORED HASSAN'S MOOD.

roots deep into the earth to find his. But when Sitha tugged at Hassan's roots, she found they were not fixed. He was beginning to loosen his grip on the island. Sitha could feel that he was vulnerable.

Hassan sagged further towards the water. A grey heron zipped ashore on the salty air, eager to get ahead of the weather. With it, an idea came to Sitha.

"Bird-friend!" She called to the grey heron.

"Yes, Little Palm?" the heron replied.

"Come and sit with me. I need your help," Sitha invited.

The heron came to rest atop Sitha's leaves.

"You see the strong elder beside me? He has lost his purpose," she explained. "Can you help me? I am young and I am still learning, but you have seen many things."

The grey heron nodded, accepting the challenge.

"Uncle Palm!" he said, turning to the elder tree. "Your leaves are the island's very reason for being. I come and go, but you remain here steadfastly. I'll prove it. Follow my path," the grey heron proclaimed and lifted into the sky.

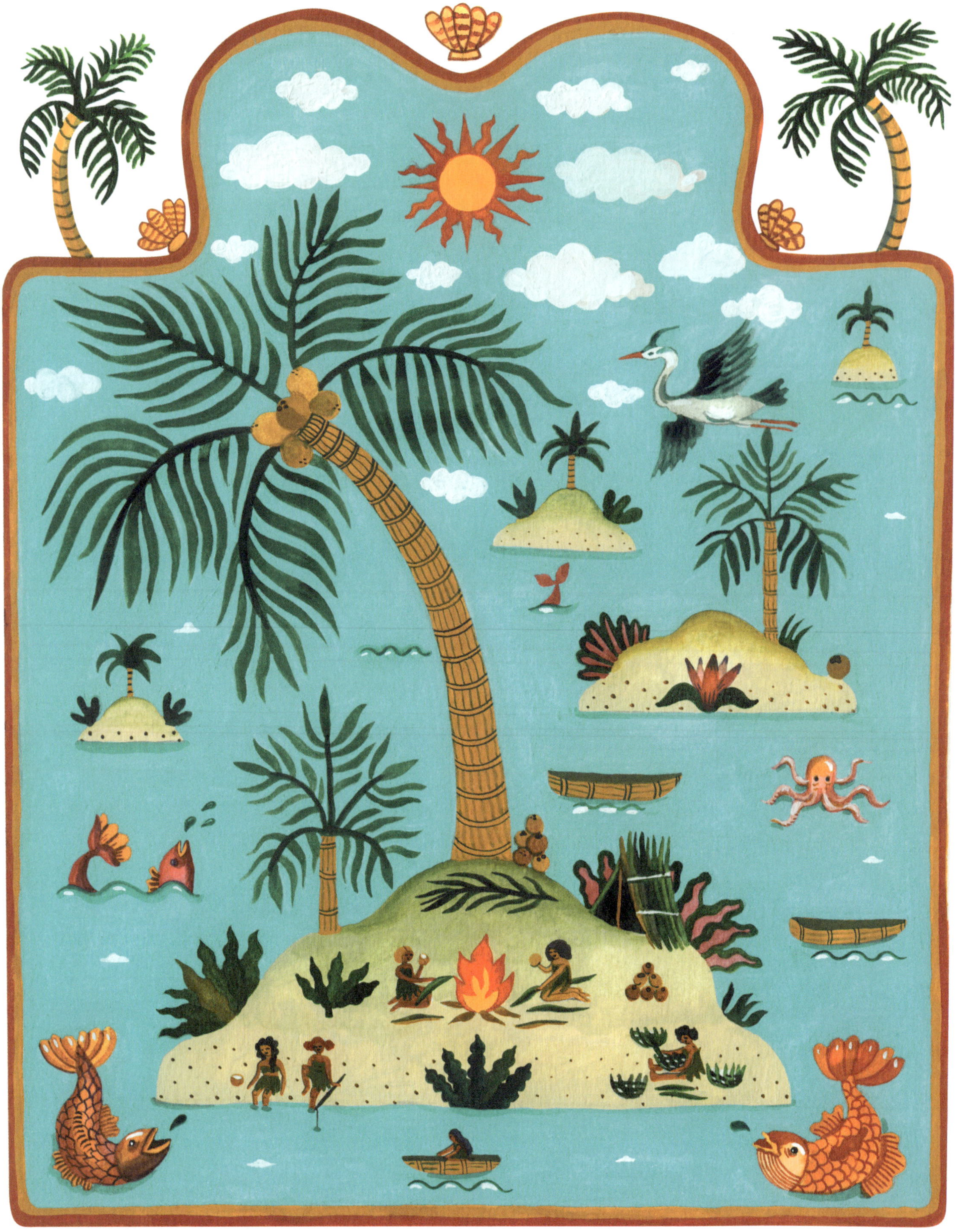

Sitha nudged Hassan out of his funk.

"Hassan, do you see that grey heron?" she called to Hassan, who shrugged. "He is going to take us on a tour."

First, the grey heron flew to a market lined with stalls. There, the island's people were cooling off after a day of hustle in the steamy sun. They could be seen quenching their thirst with milk from mature coconuts. They slipped through the smiling face holes at the top, then cracked open the shell and scooped out the tissue to fill their bellies. The coconut was the centrepiece of their days end relief.

"See here?" the grey heron called to the trees. "Those coconuts fell from your branches."

"Look!" said Sitha, impressed. She shook her fledgling branches in Hassan's direction. "Your coconuts mean something."

Hassan looked briefly but turned back to the water. The waves grew as the storm neared. The grey heron zoomed between the trees and the duo watched as the bird swooped near a small boat. Sitha leaned over the water to get a better look and saw that the boat was made from palms much like her and Hassan's. The unmistakable pattern of the trunk was carved with seagoing designs. Sitha beamed up at Hassan. He humoured her and nodded.

> "LOOK!" SAID SITHA, IMPRESSED. SHE SHOOK HER FLEDGLING BRANCHES IN HASSAN'S DIRECTION. "YOUR COCONUTS MEAN SOMETHING."

The grey heron followed the vessel as it disembarked, and its sailors carried bundles ashore. They strode to a spot on the beach where fallen palm leaves had been collected and stacked together to form a shelter. The sailors gathered under its protection as the storm's first raindrops landed.

The sailors dug a nook in the sand and layered cut wood with dried leaves and their catch from the sea. Soon it was alit and warming them all. More islanders joined, with open coconuts, herbs and plants in generous baskets woven from palm leaves.

"Well, would you look at that?" Sitha marvelled.

"It does look festive," Hassan had to admit.

The rain became a downpour, but the assembled islanders remained dry in the shelter. They laid their offerings on the fire, and soon savoury, smoky, spicy and sweet smells, filled the air. Little ones ran to huddle close to the fire and take the first bites of the cooked fish. The grey heron, knowing they were messy eaters, lingered for morsels that he might snap up.

In spite of the merriment the storm still beset the little island. As it arrived in full, Hassan nearly returned to the doldrums. The grey heron let out a squawk to keep his attention. And Hassan looked closely at the scene before him. He saw that the island inhabitants did not retreat, instead, they carried on with their feast under the palm leaf shelter. Something came over him, and Hassan quietly held fast too.

When the thunder was loud, the little ones were scared. One of the inhabitants took out a whistle and a toy figure. They danced the figure in one hand and played on the whistle with the other. The little ones laughed. Even the grey heron danced along.

The evening wore on and when the storm lost its energy, a gentle pitter-patter of rain became background music. Stars showed themselves in the early night sky and a new mood took over the inhabitants.

As the little ones became sleepy, the fire died down leaving rosy embers. The islanders formed a tight circle with a singular focal point. It was one of their elders.

Oil was poured from a coconut into seashells and lit from the ends of the fire to create luminaires. They read like stars on the sand. The elder islander took a palm broom in one hand and swept the area in front of them. They then took a shell and drew a story in the wet sand.

All eyes were on this one wise storyteller. Hassan became immersed in their tale. The story told of the great palm tree who delivered everything necessary to make the island a home. The elder drew a towering tree and as they worked, gestured at Hassan, the model and inspiration for their story.

Sitha looked to Hassan too. His quietness had changed from that of foreboding to something softer, warmer. Sitha could feel his roots stretch beside her own – a great yawn in preparation for a pleasant rest.

When the story was over, the inhabitants of the island dispersed from the palm pavilion. The elder was the last to leave. They extinguished the lamps and poured the coconut oil from the shells into their hair. Sitha and Hassan watched as the elder combed the coconut oil in. It brought a shine to their hair so strong that the moon was reflected.

The elder then kneaded the remaining coconut oil on their skin and into their muscles. They stretched tall like a tree and grew a whole inch before their eyes! They reached wide like a palm leaf and their limbs moved with elegant ease. And when they went on their way, Hassan, Sitha and the grey heron saw a spring in their step usually reserved to one much younger.

Sitha turned to Hassan, ready to pepper him with ideas and happy observations. But instead, Hassan hushed her with his own thoughts.

"I see now, Little Palm; we coconut trees are more than our fruits and flowers. We are more than materials and pieces... We are the centre for those who also call our island their home. We must stay here as long as they are here."

Sitha bent her trunk beneath his. The grey heron rested on top.

"Their story is *our* story, Little Palm. It belongs to all of us," said Hassan.

ONCE UPON A REEF

Thousands of years ago, along a great peninsula that stretched from the mainland into a warm ocean, lived two brothers. They weren't a typical family; one was a seagull and the other a whale, but they were family to each other, nonetheless, linked by a chance meeting far out in the ocean.

Whale, a young calf, had travelled a great distance, practicing their natural navigation skills. High above, Gull, too, had travelled far, using the colourful water below to track their path.

"Aero, Azure, Sea Foam, Pale Blue, Aqua, Turquoise, Teal," Gull recited.

On that particular day, lava vents near the water had suddenly become active and smoke turned the clear skies into a heavy haze. Gull's vision was instantly clouded, and they could no longer see the colourful waters to chart their way. Flummoxed, Gull flew in circles. Fear quickly descended upon the lost bird.

THEY COULD NO LONGER SEE THE COLOURFUL WATERS TO CHART THEIR WAY.

Below, deep in the water, away from the smoke and bluster, swam young Whale. When they surfaced for a breath, Whale heard a kerfuffle above them – a flurry of flaps and a terrible squawk. It was, of course, Gull. Whale puffed a spray of water and called out to a confused seabird, "You, up there! Are you lost?"

"Terribly!" replied the panicked Gull.

"Not to worry!" Whale said confidently. "I am a keen navigator. I will show you the way."

"But how? I cannot see!" Gull replied, worried.

"Listen! You will hear my breaths," Whale reassured the stranger in the sky.

Sure enough, attentive Gull was calmed by the rhythm of Whale's breathing.

"Follow my lead," Whale called up.

Gull followed the breath in and out. The rhythm became a guiding signal from the sea. Gull followed Whale all the way to clear skies – and to safety. Gull was overcome with joy and gratitude and vowed to return the favour someday.

"No need," Whale responded.

"Well, you'll always have my friendship then," Gull offered.

GULL FOLLOWED WHALE ALL THE WAY TO CLEAR SKIES – AND TO SAFETY.

From that day forward, Whale and Gull had an instant and lasting bond.

They spent days devising parallel fun. Gull swooped and skimmed the water near Whale. Whale would breach, spray and chase down their pal. While Whale left for colder waters every year, they returned to the same spot where they had first met Gull. Over time, the two came to call one another 'brother'. The peninsula and the surrounding waters were their shared haven.

The brothers travelled among and above the water's wonderous coral and wildlife; fish, rays, sea stars and crustaceans in all colours and shapes. There was plenty for the pals to explore. As the two grew older, so did the coral community. It matured to enclose the peninsula like a halo.

Whale and Gull loved this coral halo and spent much of their time there. Their friendship inspired other plants and animals to call the coral their home and in time, the halo became a packed reef. A reliable home to generations of countless creatures – great and small.

Whale and Gull were the reef's mascots, unofficial captains of the neighbourhood. They were a constant presence above can beneath and helped any animals they met to find their way. Gull of course guided the new arrivals through the waters; "Aero, Azure, Sea Foam, Pale Blue, Aqua, Turquoise, Teal!"

One year, near the end of winter, something strange began to happen. The sea vents, which had been dormant since Gull and Whale's first chance meeting, began to swell and sputter. At first, their emissions were few, just small jets of steam. But soon, the discharges grew more regular – and, at times, the mainland and the peninsula would shift and slide and quake beside the reef.

THE WARMER WATERS HAD CAUSED THE REEF TO ACT IN MYSTERIOUS WAYS.

Whale nestled in growing waves and the warmth that jetted below. They tried to comfort and reassure the nervous residents of the reef. Gull, meanwhile, spent time overhead collecting information to share with Whale below.

From above, Gull could see that other changes were taking place too. The warmer waters had caused the reef to act in mysterious ways. Gull saw that some of the wildlife ebbed away and the coral had taken on new and ghostly hues.

"The water has changed!" remarked Whale as the brothers journeyed alongside the peninsula, Gull atop Whale's back.

"Yes," agreed Gull. "From the sky, all the colours are different."

"Have you noticed the animals are moving away?' asked Whale.

"Yes, I have," Gull said anxiously. "Will you come back next winter, brother?"

"Oh, I'll be back, don't worry," Whale replied. But both brothers sensed uncertainty.

As the weeks wore on, winter drew to a close, and soon it was time for Whale to depart. By then, the reef had grown even more irregular. Whale was reluctant to leave.

"What if I stayed? Whale suggested. "Perhaps I could convince other animals and algae to return, to bring the colour back to the reef?"

Gull saw from their vantage point that the reef was nearly white, and that little movement could be found in among the coral.

"I don't know... It could be too late," Gull agonized.

"It's worth trying!" Whale said defiantly, and quickly dove beneath the water. Gull watched Whale head purposefully towards the reef.

Suddenly, a resounding *BOOM!* was heard, and at the spot where the peninsula attached to the mainland, a great fissure opened in the earth. Fiery rocks shot forth from the opening. Ribbons of black smoke bloomed behind the projectiles. Gull knew the air would be thick with smoke before long and they sped past the edge of the peninsula to the far reaches of the bereft reef.

Gull swooped and searched the water for Whale. Behind them, the land exploded and roared. Enflamed lava spilled from higher ground and ran to the water's edge. Gull feared for Whale. As the hot lava runoff hit the saltwater, it fizzed and steamed and formed bulbous rocks. It looked like a burned border between land and sea.

Gull took to a safe height and looked down. In a dark pathway between the peninsula and the reef, Gull spotted Whale trapped among the new black rocks which had formed a wall. Whale was coming up for frequent breaths but had little room to manoeuvre. Gull

GULL SPOTTED WHALE TRAPPED AMONG THE NEW BLACK ROCKS WHICH HAD FORMED A WALL.

remembered the day they had met — when Whale was calm and reassuring and had shepherded Gull to safety.

Gull plummeted towards the water, calling to Whale, "I've got you, brother!"

Gull scarcely knew what to do, until they spotted trees that had been upended by the trembling land. They flew to them and grabbed some branches in their bill. With all their might, Gull dragged the trees one by one to where the peninsula met the mainland.

Moving each tree scored and cut the earth beneath. And scored and cut Gull's mouth. But Gull dragged and pulled the trees until the land beneath was etched and soft. Whale was coming up more frequently for air; Gull monitored their sea spray anxiously.

As the mainland let loose a final forceful blast, Gull pulled one last tree across the ground. When the trees scraped the soil a final time, the peninsula and the reef parted from the mainland in an epic break.

At the place where Whale had been stuck, a gateway opened. Whale breached high in the air, over the black rocks, and landed heavily in the water before heading out into the ocean. Gull flew above Whale. Behind them, their home, their haven, was blanketed in smoke and ash.

The brothers looked back at their former home from a safe distance.

"Will the reef recover?" Whale mourned. "Will it ever be a home again?"

From deep within, Gull found optimism and reserve. "We'll follow the colours," he said. "They will take us to a vibrant new home."

"The colours?" Whale asked.

"This way," Gull flew ahead.

"Aero, Azure, Sea Foam, Pale Blue, Aqua, Turquoise, Teal," Gull recited. "When the reef has recovered, we will follow the colours home."

Together they travelled onward, brothers bonded by the sea. Together they held fast to the promise of a day when the reef would once again be a place of splendour, majesty and colour: a place they could call home.

ONCE UPON THE TOP OF THE WORLD

Spruce, spruce, spruce, spruce. That is what Picea needed for their family, for their home and for their future. Spruce for building, spruce for cooking, spruce for heating, spruce for shade. Even the spruce beetles which fell from the trees were the perfect Picea snack.

Picea's stomach rumbled. They rubbed their hairy pelt. Picea could not stop for a snack. They had to keep going.

Picea was a unique being. High as the tallest bear, but with half as much fur. Picea had a big, round head like a melon, but a face that was soft and smiley. Picea had short legs, yet long arms. And their hands and feet were the size of fat and furry raccoons.

Within their perhaps irregular appearance, Picea was a steadfast and caring creature. Which was good, because they needed

PICEA WAS A STEADFAST AND CARING CREATURE.

both qualities on their quest for spruce. Picea and their kinfolk needed spruce for all things. They needed spruce for medicine when they happened on hard times. They needed spruce for happy occasions when good times befell them. And they especially needed spruce to brush their big teeth!

With not a spruce in sight, Picea had to keep moving. Picea needed to first hear a steady *Crunch, Crunch!* beneath their big padded feet. Then an audible *Thump!* which meant that beneath the spruce needles lay firm and stable ground. Ground of that sound had become increasingly harder for Picea and their kinfolk to depend on.

You see, Picea's homeport was built on a spot appointed by their ancestors tens of thousands of years before. Ancestors who had come to the land by way of a bridge. A long slice of land that stretched across white-sheeted icy waters and joined two larger lands. Now, Picea's home, once firm and sturdy, had become very soggy.

The change had happened without notice, slowly, over a long time. It began with heavier rains and an intruding marsh. Mushrooms appeared where they had not before. Year after year, deluges came earlier and lingered longer. The wet conditions sloshed and logged Picea's homeport.

After a while, every step that Picea and her kinfolk took made a sucking noise. The town's once-sturdy spruce forest had slowly sunk into the mud. And when they planted new spruce needles, they just washed away.

NOW, PICEA'S HOME, ONCE FIRM AND STURDY, HAD BECOME VERY SOGGY.

Then one day, Picea went to close the door to the storehouse that held their last precious spruce needles, which had, by now, become covered in mushrooms. It would not move. It was held in the mud. That was when Picea knew they would need to move.

Picea's ancestors had once gone in search of a new home. Now it was their turn.

This undertaking came with great risk. When Picea's ancestors had crossed the bridge, there were others already at home on the other side. They had tried not to interrupt the existing way of life, but their size, their form and their fur alarmed the residents. They mistook Picea's kind for beasts and fled.

Ever since, Picea and their kinfolk had been careful to stay secluded, keeping themselves to themselves. Their search for a new home had to be done with secrecy too. Picea had to hide in the trees or hold very still when they feared they might be detected.

At last, after walking and listening, dodging and hiding, Picea reached a place of higher ground. They felt beneath their feet the reassuring *Crunch!* of spruce needles when they walked. They jumped and – *Thump!* – strong, sturdy ground held firm.

Picea could see their mud-sunken homeport far in the distance. The new spot where they stood was up a steep ascent, but it was essential that they move here. Picea knew it – all they had to do was show their kinfolk. To prove the viability of the new location, Picea grabbed armfuls of spruce needles and began the steep journey down towards home.

PICEA HUGGED THE SPRUCE NEEDLES WITH ALL THEIR MIGHT.

At first, Picea's descent was slow and purposeful. Spruce needles drifted from their gentle arms as they trekked cautiously onwards. Picea calculated each careful step so that their large frame didn't topple head over foot. But they stumbled, and spruce needles sprayed out in bursts.

After a while, the conditions began to change, and Picea's concern was no longer stumbling, but slipping. The rocks were wet with moisture from the lowlands. Boulders that looked secure slid in soft mud. Picea hugged the spruce needles with all their might. The long barbs wove into their fur. Tiny spikes dug into their skin.

The journey was nearly half-completed and the day's end was near. Picea bent over, keeping low to the ground as they continued their decent. Soon the night animals would appear and Picea needed to be out of sight.

Picea hurried, but judged a foothold poorly and slid into a full split. Their arms stretched out to support them and the bulk of spruce needles shot into the air like

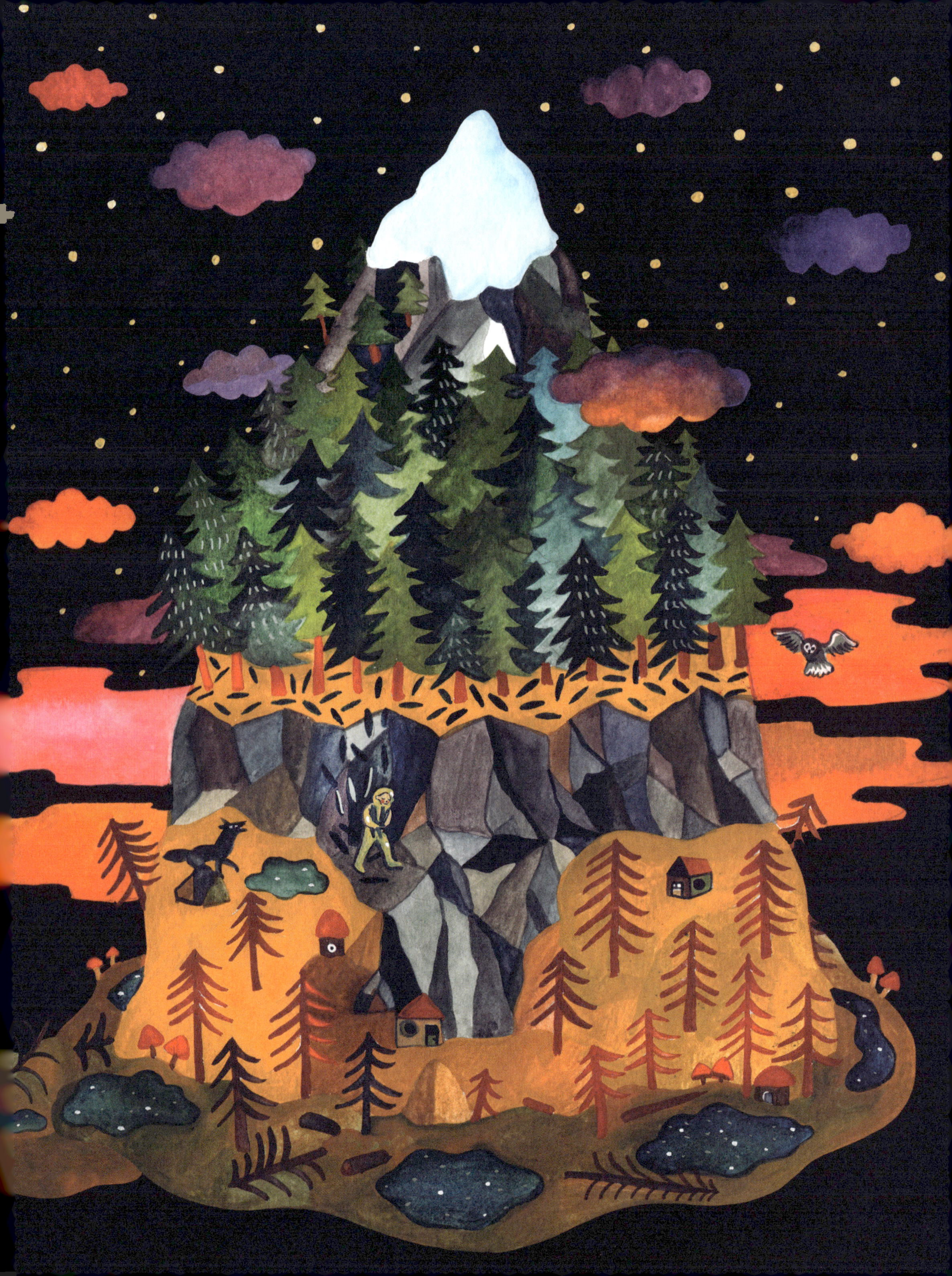

confetti. Alone in the darkness, sore, mud-caked, with little to show for their efforts, Picea wanted to give up. Their bounty of spruce needles was sadly depleted in the blundering descent. As Picea reached the end of the journey, they held only a few spruce needles to show for their efforts.

Picea scooped mud into their oversized hands in order to seal the last few needles to their palm. Then, hand over hand, they crawled to the centre of their homeport. Wincing and flinching, Picea stood, hands outstretched, in invitation to their kinfolk to join them. Soon came the sound of a hundred feet sucking and flopping through the mud. It rang like a clumsy applause.

The kinfolk gathered near and examined Picea.

"Only mud," someone said with a sigh as they brushed the dirt from poor Picea's pelt.

"We're doomed," another grunted, bringing Picea a woven blanket to warm them.

"We'll go extinct, like our drowned spruce forest," someone whispered.

"Our sources for everything – lost!" someone worried aloud.

"We will lose ourselves," someone said tearfully, and took Picea by the hand. As they did, the mud dropped away from Picea's hands and the few intact spruce needles were revealed.

The one holding Picea's hand lifted it high for all to see. Everyone was silent.

THE ONE HOLDING PICEA'S HAND LIFTED IT HIGH FOR ALL TO SEE.

"Are those spruce needles?" a small voice broke the hush.

Picea nodded and pointed to the high spot from which they had journeyed.

"We can relocate, but we must do it all at once, and all together," Picea explained. Their kinfolk were relieved but wary.

"It will be steep, but I have laid a path," Picea continued. Sure enough, if one looked carefully, they could see a river of spruce needles that marked the route that Picea had travelled, from high, dry ground right the way down to the soggy bottom.

There wasn't time to rejoice. All those assembled raced as quickly at the mud would allow to collect what they could carry. Building supplies, food, medicine, fabrics, leaves, seeds and vessels. All of it was piled on to shoulders and backs. Tucked under arms and balanced atop heads.

By dawn, Picea's community was ready for their big move. They lined the course and followed Picea's path. They hurried to conceal their presence before the day grew bright and busy.

When Picea saw the first of their kinfolk reach the high dry place, they made a final mark on their former land. In a gesture of gratitude and goodbye, Picea pulled a dead spruce from its post in the mud and upturned it so the roots reached for the sky. Picea continued this way, until all the lifeless trees of the area held this new orientation. Then, with a gentle bow to the spruce ghosts, Picea ascended the

PICEA ASCENDED THE SPRUCE NEEDLE PATH TO BEGIN THEIR NEW LIFE IN A NEW HOME.

spruce needle path to begin their new life in a new home.

In the years that followed, the spruce needle path disappeared. In its place grew a massive new forest. A forest that kept secret Picea and their kinfolk, and kept them flourishing.

As for the land below, water took over and transformed it into a lush wetland. The upturned trees grew thick with moss and lichen. Ferns and mushrooms carpeted the land, and all who passed were certain that wonderful beings had once called it home.

ONCE UPON A TUNDRA

Atop our planet sits a magnificent crown. Its band is made of tundra that reaches far and wide. Its regal arches are formed by mossy rocks. It is bejewelled with fragrant herbs and flowering wilds that sneak out between deep cold and gentle thaw.

This precious apex was once home to an epic rescue squad. The group included a caribou named Sunflower, a polar bear called Aurora, an owl called Willow and a fox named Peat. This is their story.

The four animals – Sunflower, Aurora, Willow and Peat – were never thought to cross paths. Sunflower the caribou grazed on grasslands and enjoyed the company of a massive herd. Aurora the polar bear slid on snowy slopes and splashed in dark waters. Willow the owl spent their days high above in stealth – a shrewd witness. By contrast, Peat the fox slunk between tall legs, dove in the snow and lived life as a game of tag, wary not to be caught out.

One brisk day, a rumble rolled across the tundra. It shook the berries from bushes, the leaves off trees and forced the pollen from the grasses in a green cloud. The rumble woke burrowed animals; it sent winged ones into flight and those in the water turned to the depths. The sound was made by the mighty advance of a herd of caribou. Among them was the first of our foursome, Sunflower.

WILLOW HAD SEEN THE HERD PACE BY AND WONDERED WHY ONE CARIBOU REMAINED.

Sunflower was named for a great sunburst patch on her shoulders. She stood tall and fuzzy and was a dreamer. Around her, the herd surged. With urgency and vigour, they powered across the land. But Sunflower dawdled distractedly, and when the dust of a thousand hooves cleared, Sunflower lingered alone.

Above Sunflower soared Willow the owl who knew well the path of grasses and shrubs. Each tree was a point on a great map in her mind. Willow had seen the herd pace by and wondered why one caribou remained. Willow found a thermal current to lift her higher. From a new height, she saw the reason for the herd's hasty departure.

Willow beheld a growing cloud as white as her own feathers. Its odour was as strong as a wall

▸ 68 ◂

and it filled Willow's mouth like chalk. Willow was wise; she had flown the tundra for many years and she knew that the cloud meant fire.

Willow understood that every now and again, the land reset and went to sleep. It did so by drawing over itself a blanket of fire. When fire was called for, the animals listened and got out of the way. From above, Willow could see that this was the young caribou's first experience with fire. Instead of departing with her herd, the worried owl watched on as Sunflower moseyed, unaware of the great danger that drew ever closer. Willow knew she had to do something before the fire arrived.

Willow called to the lone daydreamer below with her raspy whistle. Sunflower heard it right away and perked up her ears.

"Who's there?" asked Sunflower.

"Look up!" Willow replied. Sunflower looked above and saw the owl swooping low.

"Why haven't you followed your herd?" Not waiting for an answer, Willow went on. "There is a fire coming to sweep this area anew! You must keep moving," she urged.

"A fire? What's that?" Sunflower sniffed the air innocently.

"Fire is a powerful force that extinguishes everything that draws breath."

Sunflower became fearful.

"Fire comes infrequently," explained Willow, "but when it does, we must all make way for it!"

Willow flew ahead and saw that the herd was well out of view.

"Follow me. I can navigate from here." Willow made like an arrow in the sky so that Sunflower could trail her.

Sunflower threaded shrubs, rocks and trees until they arrived at a great bouldery expanse. Running in a state of blind agitation, Sunflower barrelled right into a line of stone, knocking her knees badly. A pain ran through her and she toppled over, shivering. It was unclear where to go. In one direction she saw advancing flames. In the other, a wall of smoke progressed. Sunflower had nowhere to go but directly forwards through the challenging terrain ahead.

"We are going to need eyes on the ground," Willow said, letting out a long whistle-cry.

A rustling sound was heard between rocks and a sleek fox slid into view atop a rock – like the star of his very own show.

"Peat is here!" the Fox announced. "To whom do I owe the pleasure?"

The owl presented the young caribou.

"My herd left without me – I was distracted," Sunflower admitted, "and now I can't find a path safely away from the fire."

"Follow me!" Peat, an expert on rocky terrain, bounded nimbly from rock to rock, and led Sunflower up ramps, down hidden courses and through tunnels. The caribou had to stoop in spots, got bumped in others and took countless scrapes, but she persisted.

All the while, Willow soared above and monitored the fire behind them. But suddenly a new predicament appeared ahead. A stretch of water lay before the group. And behind them the crescent of fire encircled.

At the water, the trio looked ahead and behind. Each of them knew there was no alternative.

> IT WAS UNCLEAR WHERE TO GO. IN ONE DIRECTION SHE SAW ADVANCING FLAMES. IN THE OTHER, A WALL OF SMOKE PROGRESSED.

"We must swim!" shouted Peat, diving in confidently.

Sunflower flinched. She did not jump in after Peat. The boulders and branches had cut into Sunflower's velvet coat. Climbing had made her joints sore. Ducking into tunnels had injured her antlers. She waded into the water and paddled poorly, wincing with each stroke. The icy waters stung.

Midway into the swim, Sunflower's muscles began to quake. Her legs began to seize and no longer moved at her command. Her head dipped below the water. She gasped for air and tried to surge on, but it was too hard. Sunflower began to sink into the water.

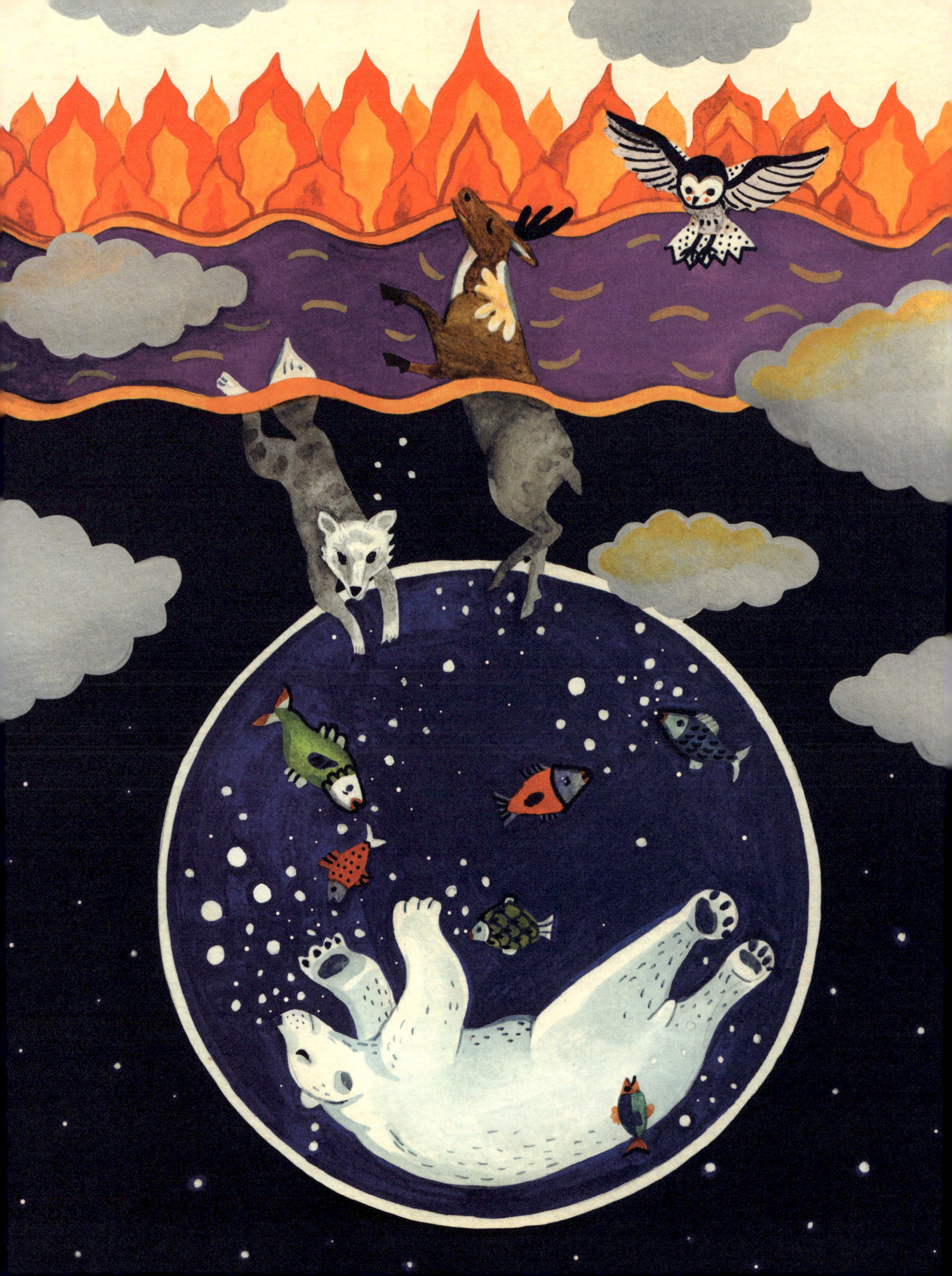

Willow called to Peat, "She needs more help!"

Peat swam alongside Sunflower and wrapped his tail around her shoulders.

"Keep going, Sunflower! You can make it!" he cheered her on. "The fire cannot reach the other side."

Willow flew ahead. "I can see your herd!" she called back. "They've found safety!" she reported.

Sunflower fought to keep her head above the water, but Willow and Peat could both see that the young caribou couldn't go any further without help.

"Peat, we need extra help. Summon Aurora!" Willow urged.

Peat froze. Peat and Aurora were natural enemies. Growing up, Peat had learned that Aurora's kind were to be feared. That they were ruthless and ferocious. Willow could see that Peat hesitated.

"Peat, you must put aside your past grudges. Go and get Aurora!" Willow repeated, adding with a powerful shriek. "She is Sunflower's only chance."

> "PEAT, WE NEED EXTRA HELP. SUMMON AURORA!" WILLOW URGED.

Willow's shriek reverberated across the water, catching the attention of the caribou herd ahead. They peered out across the waters and were horrified to see one of their youngest members in such a dire situation.

Peat took a long look at the pitiful caribou and resolved to do whatever he could to help. He dove into water. Far below, he could see Aurora the polar bear. She glided through the water with elegant power. She didn't look ruthless or stealthy or ferocious. She was spinning and blowing bubbles playfully with the fish.

Peat zipped around Aurora to get her attention and gestured to Sunflower's flailing form above them. Aurora quickly grasped the situation. The pair ascended together in a powerful surge of white fur and propelled Sunflower upwards just as her head slipped beneath the waters.

Peat wrapped himself around Sunflower's shoulders while Aurora swam beneath her like a raft and lifted the caribou's exhausted body. Together, the three swam towards the herd assembled on the far shore.

> PEAT WRAPPED HIMSELF AROUND SUNFLOWER'S SHOULDERS WHILE AURORA SWAM BENEATH HER LIKE A RAFT AND LIFTED THE CARIBOU'S EXHAUSTED BODY.

At last, Sunflower, Aurora and Peat reached the land, a tired, panting pile of wet fur. Willow announced their landing with a fly over before landing on the ground beside Sunflower. Aurora rolled on to her feet, and tenderly dried Sunflower with her own double-layered coat. Peat watched on and his fear of polar bears fell away, like beads of water, from his mind.

Gathered on the banks, they all watched as the fire burned across the water. The foursome silently looked from one to the other. They rested their heads together and made a promise: to keep the animals of the tundra safe – by becoming a rescue squad. A team that would be ever ready to shepherd animals to safety – by land, by water and by air – whenever their prized land needed to be reborn.

ONCe UPoN a RIVeRBANK

A grandmother Grasshopper and granddaughter Grasshopper sat together on a tall blade of grass. It bowed under their weight in an arc. The grass was in a field. The field was beside a river. The river snaked a trail through a peninsula between two cold seas.

"Grandmother, it's time I had my own patch of grass!" Granddaughter Grasshopper said.

"Not so fast, Little Hopper!" said Grandmother Grasshopper, blocking the request.

"But everyone else has their own patch," the youngster whined. "When will I get mine?"

"There is no extra grass to be had," said Grandmother Grasshopper finally.

"But when spring arrives so do the grasses, right, Grandmother?" Granddaughter Grasshopper reasoned.

"Yes, but so does the mud. The land slips and slides and each spring there are fewer places for the grass to grow," Grandmother Grasshopper explained.

"Oh," said Granddaughter Grasshopper sadly. But then she brightened as she said, "I know! We can ask Nature for a little extra grass, just for me. And never ask for anything ever again!"

"Don't you know the story of our Ancestor Grasshopper and her friend Beetle?" asked Grandmother Grasshopper.

"No, did they get their own grass?" Granddaughter Grasshopper asked.

"No," Grandmother Grasshopper explained. "I'll tell you their tale. Your great-great-Ancestor Grasshopper became friends with Beetle in spite of having very little in common. Our ancestor – with her bendy legs and distance jumping – and the tiny beetle – with his hard shell and face in the dirt – were the best of pals."

"Really?" Granddaughter Grasshopper was flabbergasted. "*They* were friends?"

"Truly. The two even made a special agreement that they would never leave each other's side and do everything together. Which, as you can imagine, was a doomed prospect," Grandmother Grasshopper laughed.

"Oh no, is this a scary story?" worried Granddaughter Grasshopper.

"Just listen. One day, the two set out on an adventure. Straight away, they encountered a stream. Following Ancestor Grasshopper, who easily jumped across, Beetle waded out to the edge of some slippery rocks but was swept into the water."

"Ah, I don't like how this story is going," Granddaughter Grasshopper said anxiously.

"Don't fret," Grandmother Grasshopper continued. "Your Ancestor Grasshopper was a smart and steadfast friend. She called to Beetle to grab hold of something while she jumped to find help. The first creature she came to was a boar. She asked the boar if she could have a bristle from his snout to reach out to Beetle and save him from the water."

"Did the boar help her?" Granddaughter Grasshopper asked hopefully.

"The boar said he'd be glad to help but would need an acorn in return. He had not eaten for many days and needed help of his own you see," Grandmother Grasshopper explained.

"Did Ancestor Grasshopper get an acorn?" the younger pressed.

"Our Ancestor Grasshopper hurried to the oak tree to ask for an acorn. She explained to the tree that if she could just get one extra acorn to give to the boar then he would give a bristle, and with the bristle she could save her friend Beetle from drowning," the elder continued.

"Phew," Granddaughter Grasshopper said, relieved.

"Not so fast," Grandmother Grasshopper replied. "The oak tree had her own needs. She couldn't give away her fruits for free. The tree explained that she had been beset upon by thieving birds who took more than their share of nuts, and so she asked Ancestor Grasshopper to scare them off."

"Ancestor Grasshopper bounded to the birds and said, 'Please leave the oak tree alone! I need the oak tree to give me her acorns, so that I may give one to the boar, so that they will give me a bristle, so that I may save my drowning friend, Beetle!'"

"What did the birds say?" pressed Granddaughter Grasshopper.

"The birds were empathetic, but they too had their own struggle. They said that weasels pestered them and that if Ancestor Grasshopper could get the weasels to leave them be then they would let up on the oak tree. The oak tree could then spare an acorn which could be brought to the boar to obtain a bristle and save Beetle."

"I suppose the weasels had needs too?" Granddaughter Grasshopper sighed.

"Of course, my dear, all creatures have needs," smiled Grandmother Grasshopper. "The weasels needed eggs. So Ancestor Grasshopper went to the chickens. But the chickens needed corn. So Ancestor Grasshopper hopped to the bags of corn. But she found the bags had been nibbled by mice!"

"So Ancestor Grasshopper sought the mice?" Granddaughter Grasshopper grasped.

"You got it! And of course, the mice had needs too.

They needed the cat to leave them be. But the cat needed cream from the cows," Grandmother Grasshopper grew breathless as she described the circle. "The cows needed grass and water to replenish their cream supply. And this final request by the cows for grasses and water lead Ancestor Grasshopper back to the stream where dear Beetle was still hanging on for his life!"

"What did the stream say?" asked Granddaughter Grasshopper urgently.

"First, Ancestor Grasshopper explained to the water, 'Oh waters of life! Give me wet grass, please! The grass I shall give to the cow, then the cow will give the cats cream, then the cats will stop worrying the mice, then the mice will stop eating the corn, then the chickens can eat corn and give eggs to the weasels, then the weasels will stop pestering the birds, then the birds will leave the oak tree, then the oak tree will give acorns to the boar, then the boar will give me a bristle and with this bristle I may save my drowning friend, whose feet are in your rushing waters!'"

"And did the stream help?" Granddaughter Grasshopper demanded.

"The waters of the stream relented. They gave the wet grass so Ancestor Grasshopper could obtain the bristle from the boar and she raced to save her friend."

"And so Beetle was safe!" sighed Granddaughter Grasshopper, relieved.

"No, indeed," Grandmother Grasshopper paused to give her granddaughter's feelings some space. "Beetle was nowhere to be found!"

"What?" exclaimed Granddaughter Grasshopper.

"The stream had a message for Ancestor Grasshopper instead. It said, 'All things on earth exist together in a circle. You cannot ask more of one creature, or of nature's wonders, without asking a little extra of all of them.' When the voice of the stream had finished, Ancestor Grasshopper saw that it had gently rescued Beetle and placed him safely on the bank."

Granddaughter Grasshopper breathed a sigh of relief.

"All things exist in a continuous shared chain. We call this reciprocity," Grandmother Grasshopper explained.

"I see," Granddaughter Grasshopper reflected. "So if I want my own patch of grass, I must be willing to do something extra for all the things that exist in a chain with the grass."

"Yes, you see it clearly my dear," Grandmother Grasshopper nodded. "Our circle is vast; we must do no less than that which is asked of us and take no more than we need."

And with that, the two generations of grasshoppers swayed contently on their blades of grass; the legacy of their ancestor hung in the air and the sound of the stream ran softly nearby.

To the young leaders, shifting the culture,
and planting new seeds —VM

MAGIC CAT PUBLISHING

Once Upon Our Planet © 2021 Magic Cat Publishing Ltd
Text © 2021 Vita Murrow
Illustrations © 2021 Aitch
First Published in 2021 by Magic Cat Publishing Ltd
The Milking Parlour, Old Dungate Farm, Plaistow Road, Dunsfold, Surrey GU8 4PJ, UK

The right of Vita Murrow to be identified as the author of this work and Aitch to be identified as the illustrator of this work has been asserted by them in accordance with the Copyright, Designs and Patents Act, 1988 (UK).

No part of this publication may be reproduced, stored in a retrieval system, or transmitted, in any form, or by any means, electrical, mechanical, photocopying, recording or otherwise without the prior written permission of the publisher or a licence permitting restricted copying.

A catalogue record for this book is available from the British Library.

ISBN 978-1-913520-08-3

The illustrations were created with watercolour and gouache paint
Set in Apercu, Green Narcu and Yeseva One

Published by Rachel Williams and Jenny Broom
Designed by Nicola Price

Manufactured in China, TLF0321

9 8 7 6 5 4 3 2 1

FSC MIX Paper from responsible sources FSC® C104723

VITA MURROW is an educator, writer and artist. Her recent feminist fairy tale retellings *High Five to the Hero* and *Power to the Princess* were celebrated as "Brilliant" by *Kirkus Reviews*. Together with her husband, artist Ethan Murrow, Vita is co-creator of the short film *Dust* (official selection in the 46th annual New York Film Festival). The Murrows children's book debut, *The Whale* was nominated for a CILIP Greenway Medal. Their recent title *Zero Local* has been nominated for a 2021 ALSC Notable Children's Book award.

Nomadic AITCH originally hails from Romania but prefers not to put down roots in any one place; new scenery inspires and invigorates her tactile, hand-rendered illustrations and a constant string of exhibitions in cities across the continent pushes her technique further. Her dreamy characters hide amongst William Morris-esque gardens and bring to mind a bright and bold reincarnation of Victorian melancholy while still retaining a strong sense of her Romanian heritage.